NEW DIRECTIONS FOR STUDENT SERVICES

Margaret J. Barr, *Northwestern University*
EDITOR-IN-CHIEF

M. Lee Upcraft, *The Pennsylvania State University*
ASSOCIATE EDITOR

Ethics for Today's Campus: New Perspectives on Education, Student Development, and Institutional Management

Jane Fried
Central Connecticut State University

EDITOR

Number 77, Spring 1997

JOSSEY-BASS PUBLISHERS
San Francisco

ETHICS FOR TODAY'S CAMPUS: NEW PERSPECTIVES ON EDUCATION,
STUDENT DEVELOPMENT, AND INSTITUTIONAL MANAGEMENT
Jane Fried (ed.)
New Directions for Student Services, no. 77
Margaret J. Barr, Editor-in-Chief
M. Lee Upcraft, Associate Editor

Microfilm copies of issues and articles are available in 16mm and 35mm,
as well as microfiche in 105mm, through University Microfilms Inc., 300
North Zeeb Road, Ann Arbor, Michigan 48106-1346.

ISSN 0164-7970   ISBN 0-7879-9857-5

NEW DIRECTIONS FOR STUDENT SERVICES is part of The Jossey-Bass Higher
and Adult Education Series and is published quarterly by Jossey-Bass Inc.,
Publishers, 350 Sansome Street, San Francisco, California 94104-1342.
Periodicals postage paid at San Francisco, California, and at additional
mailing offices. POSTMASTER: Send address changes to New Directions for
Student Services, Jossey-Bass Inc., Publishers, 350 Sansome Street, San
Francisco, California 94104-1342.

NEW DIRECTIONS FOR STUDENT SERVICES is indexed in College Student
Personnel Abstracts and Contents Pages in Education.

SUBSCRIPTIONS cost $52.00 for individuals and $79.00 for institutions,
agencies, and libraries. See Ordering Information page at end of book.

EDITORIAL CORRESPONDENCE should be sent to the Editor-in-Chief,
Margaret J. Barr, 633 Clark Street, 2-219, Evanston, Illinois 60208-1103.

Cover photograph by Wernher Krutein/PHOTOVAULT © 1990.

Manufactured in the United States of America on Lyons Falls
Pathfinder Tradebook. This paper is acid-free and 100 percent
totally chlorine-free.

CONTENTS

EDITOR'S NOTES

Professional ethics creates an imperative to consider our work in the light of its potential consequences for ourselves, our institutions, our students, and our colleagues. All professions are characterized by their willingness to establish codes of ethics and to educate and oversee practitioner compliance. On today's multicultural campuses, many ethical systems are in contact and in conflict on both personal and professional levels. This issue of *New Directions for Student Services* examines some of the emerging ethical systems that challenge or complement the system used in student affairs over the past several decades.

Ethics: Interaction and Multiculturalism

This volume is based on several assumptions about current and future student affairs practice. The first, and probably most important, is that all postsecondary education in the United States involves students, administrators, and faculty members from many cultures. In order to honor our traditional ethical principles of respecting autonomy, doing no harm, and being beneficent, just, and fair (Kitchener, 1985), ethical practice must consider the presence of different cultural perspectives on campus and use these perspectives to educational advantage whenever possible. The ethical system that dominates higher education in the United States then becomes one of many to be considered in decision making, ethical relationships, and ethics education, rather than the only valid point of view or the dominant perspective.

This multicultural and multiperspective approach presents a difficult challenge. Education, science, and U.S. culture are all based on the assumption that the best solution to or explanation for a problem relies on a single principle that is considered uniformly true across contexts. For example, equal opportunity is an important principle in the United States. Equal opportunity to attend a particular college or university might involve admission based on SAT scores and high school grade point average. Equal evaluation criteria for all applicants, in an ideal world, would yield fair admission standards. The problems with this approach have haunted higher education since the passage of Title VI in 1964, which "prohibits discrimination on the basis of race, color, or national origin in programs receiving federal assistance" (Barr, 1989, p. 93). A single principle cannot address the incredible complexity involved in determining what constitutes *equal* in the United States across lines of race, age, ethnicity, socioeconomic status, gender, or disability. People who have been trained to look for single guiding principles that lead to "right" answers may find a multiperspective approach daunting.

The second assumption is that effective ethical thinking and behavior in our complex society requires a high level of cognitive development. This assumption affects approaches both to student development and professional practice. Even supposedly simple ethical guidelines were never intended to be applied simplistically. In a multicultural setting, many ethical guidelines exist, some simple and some complex. They all interact around specific situations and must be discussed overtly (Fried, 1995). If single-principle guidelines are used covertly, misunderstandings and feelings of exclusion on the part of one or more groups are almost inevitable. Although initial conversations may be more time-consuming when multiple perspectives are solicited, the consequences of decisions made after such conversations are more likely to be widely accepted on campus.

The final assumption that shapes this volume is that the student affairs profession is profoundly involved in the fast-paced changes occurring throughout higher education because of our responsibilities for management, education, assessment, and research. As professionals, we must become familiar and comfortable with a range of ethical systems and develop innovative methods for using one or more systems to guide any set of responsibilities, working group, or learning experience. This mandate requires a lot of difficult intellectual work because of the amount of new information that must be learned and applied to practical problems. New methods of analysis and practice must be developed.

Three themes are prominent in this volume: (1) principle-centered ethics, articulated most effectively by Karen Kitchener (1985) has shaped our ethical discussions in the past decade and remains extremely important in ethical thinking; (2) feminist and relationally oriented ethics have emerged to complement principle-centered ethics. Principle-centered ethics has been criticized as too focused on autonomy and materialism (DuBose, Hamel, and O'Connell, 1994). Relational ethics emphasizes connectedness between people and connections between thinking and feeling as well as between the secular and the sacred. Virtue ethics (Meara, Schmidt, and Day, 1996) discusses characteristics of individual behavior in a community context and can also be considered relational. Dialogue is a prominent characteristic of all relational systems. (3) Stories, pictures, and poetry stimulate our intuition and present new possibilities for our ethical sensitivity. They are a valuable contribution, even though they defy traditional approaches to measurement. Several authors have referred to poets, particularly Matthew Arnold, and to story telling and picture taking. Matthew Arnold was an educator as well as a poet and wrote a great deal about education during the late eighteenth century. At that time his native country, England, was changing from an agrarian to an industrial society, causing huge shifts in cultural values and the pace and quality of life. Arnold emphasized the role of intuition and imagery in helping people understand and adjust to profound life changes. We wish to emphasize intuition, imagery, creativity, and relationships as part of the cultural and ethical transition now in progress.

Each chapter in this volume addresses one or more of the themes. In Chapter One, Jane Fried traces the historical development of our most familiar ethical system and describes some emerging systems. The principle-centered system relies on application of time-tested, universally valid principles to the resolution of problems in a hierarchical fashion. Fried discusses virtue ethics, which relies on the development of behavior patterns or virtues that are valued in specific contexts and have been used recently to cope with complex problems in biomedicine. Finally, she presents a group of values that seem to be held by students all over the world and may supply a bridge between general principles and cultural applications (Hughes, 1992). In Chapter Two, Vicki Guthrie describes the most recent research on moral development, including the *reflective judgment model,* a four-dimensional model of moral behavior, and her own research on the relationship between intellectual development and tolerance of difference. She explains in detail the processes of cognitive development that are essential to effective ethical thinking and behavior.

Chapters Three, Four, and Five discuss ethical concerns and practices in applied settings. F. J. Tally reviews the quality movement in management and its implications for ethical behavior. He explains the relationship between the processes used in quality management approaches such as involvement, self-monitoring, continuous improvement, and consensus building and the development of virtue and community-centered ethics. He suggests that dialogue and open discussion of differences offer the most effective approach to mutual respect in culturally complex communities. David Sundberg and I discuss the role of student affairs in raising ethical issues in conversations and consultations with faculty colleagues, administrators, and students. We describe several evolving roles that help build bridges across differences in institutional responsibility and cultural perspective. John Saltmarsh describes an approach to experiential education that has enormous implications for ethics education and community service learning. As a historian and philosopher, Saltmarsh describes his *learning community* approach from a slightly different perspective than student affairs professionals tend to use, but he also describes our common pedagogical roots in the beliefs of John Dewey.

Chapter Six completes the cycle of ethical awareness, thought, education, and action by presenting a holistic and visual approach to the assessment of campus climates. James Banning, who is a pioneer in the development of systemic methods for assessing campus ecology, presents his techniques for *visual anthropology.* By photographing cultural artifacts on campus and analyzing them in a three-dimensional matrix, he constructs a multidimensional, nonintrusive picture of the ethical climate on campus.

As editor, I would like to acknowledge and thank a number of other people who have contributed to this volume. Cynthia Forrest, dean of students at Framingham State College, and Janet Richardson, dean of students at Worcester Polytechnic Institute, have been particularly helpful. The master's degree students in the College Student Development program at Northeastern University have also contributed to the editor's thinking by their class participation and their willingness to discuss the ethical dilemmas they face in daily practice. Particular thanks go to Amy Sukinik, Craig Alimo, Francesca Purcell, Jana Weber, Tanya Jones, Jennifer Riddell, Megan Powers, Jennifer Sawyer, and Matthew Phillips.

Henry Kissinger is reported to have remarked, "If you don't know where you're going, any road will take you there." An updated version of this idea might be, "If you have some idea where you're going, in terms of values, ethics, and a sense of the common good, you probably will have to build your own road and you must do it with others or you won't get anywhere."

Jane Fried
Editor

References

Abrams, M. (ed.). "Matthew Arnold." In *The Norton Anthology of English Literature*. Vol. 2. New York: Norton, 1962.

Barr, M. "Legal Issues Confronting Student Affairs Practice." In U. Delworth, G. R. Hanson, and Associates (eds.), *Student Services: A Handbook for the Profession*. (2nd ed.) San Francisco: Jossey-Bass, 1989.

DuBose, E., Hamel, R., and O'Connell, L. (eds.). *A Matter of Principles? Ferment in Bioethics*. Valley Forge, Pa.: Trinity International Press, 1994.

Fried, J. *Shifting Paradigms in Student Affairs*. Washington, D.C.: American College Personnel Association, 1995.

Hughes, M. "Global Diversity and Student Development." In M. Terrell (ed.), *Diversity, Disunity, and Campus Community*. Washington, D.C.: National Association of Student Personnel Administrators, 1992.

Kitchener, K. "Ethical Principles and Ethical Decisions in Student Affairs." In H. J. Canon and R. D. Brown (eds.), *Applied Ethics in Student Services*. New Directions for Student Services, no. 30. San Francisco: Jossey-Bass, 1985.

Meara, N., Schmidt, L., and Day, J. "Principles and Virtues: A Foundation for Ethical Decisions, Policies, and Character." *The Counseling Psychologist*, 1996, 24 (1), 4–77.

JANE FRIED is associate professor in the Department of Health and Human Services at Central Connecticut State University and is former chair of the Standing Committee on Ethics of the American College Personnel Association.

The ethical principles that have guided student affairs on homogeneous campuses in more stable times must be reconsidered in the light of dramatic changes and challenges. Virtues and principles interact to provide new matrices for analysis and decision making.

Changing Ethical Frameworks for a Multicultural World

Jane Fried

"Seeing is believing" is a truism in the United States. We believe the evidence of our senses. If we see it, it must be real. Reality is so obvious that it needs no definition. Reality is synonymous with common sense. Yet anthropologist Clifford Geertz asserts that "common sense is not what the mind cleared of cant spontaneously apprehends. It is what the mind filled with presuppositions . . . concludes" (1983, p. 84). Common sense is a loosely integrated cultural system that "rests on the same basis that any other system rests on, the conviction by those whose possession it is of its value and validity" (p. 76). A more accurate rendition of the truism might be, "In the view of reality that prevails in the United States, one can trust the evidence of one's senses more than any other kind of evidence." Truisms of that length are rare and probably useless. They do not trip off the tongue at crucial moments or serve as a guide to action in confusing and difficult circumstances.

Ethical beliefs and belief systems are intended to serve as guides to action in confusing and difficult circumstances. The ethical beliefs that have influenced American culture come from a number of sources, chiefly Christianity, scientific empiricism, and a philosophical position called positivism (Fried, 1995). Positivism supports the "correspondence theory of truth," or seeing (measuring, recording, counting) is believing (Lincoln and Guba, 1985). On a mundane level, "seeing is believing" provides a very comforting approach to evaluation of truth. All the evaluation devices are, literally, in the eyes, ears, and perceptual systems of the beholder. The premise breaks down, however, when one considers docudramas, photographic manipulation of evidence, or electronic graphics that appear to be "real" but whose reality is virtual, not concrete. When one cannot identify with certainty which black and white segments are clips from history and which are created in black and white for purposes of dramatic emphasis in the films of Oliver Stone, one needs to describe reality in more complex terms than "seeing is believing." Seeing, under what circumstances, in which time frame and context, permits one to believe what, how much, in how much detail, and with what degree of commitment to the truth value of the evidence?

Making ethical judgments has never been easy. In the modern world, developing a reliable ethical perspective has become even more complicated and difficult. In the eighteenth century Benjamin Franklin wrote his ethical precepts in *Poor Richard's Almanac,* and Americans used his truisms as a guide to action for two centuries. In the nineteenth century Davy Crockett lived by a single rule: "Be sure you're right. Then go ahead." He knew what was right. How did he know? Why do we not know now? Or, more accurately, why do so many people have so many different and often conflicting ideas about what is right?

Making ethical decisions has become incredibly difficult and complicated because notions of right and good are embedded in cultural and community consensus about values. In homogeneous societies it is far easier to decide what is right than in societies that include people of many ethnic cultures. In the present multicultural society of the United States, culture can be rooted not only in ethnicity but also in common life experience and worldview related to race, socioeconomic status, professional identity, gender, sexual orientation, or disability. Most individuals are members of more than one culture, and cultural norms about good and right may vary among them.

This chapter explores the origins of the dominant, *old paradigm* ethical belief system in student affairs, which relies heavily on the application of principles to problems. Challenges to this belief system have emerged from New Paradigm thought, which incorporates ethical beliefs from many cultures and perspectives, "virtue ethics" (discussed at length later in this chapter), and the dynamic interaction between universal principles, particular situations, and individual ways of making meaning. Examples of ethical behavior in professional practice and ethics education for students will be discussed. Finally, a process for examining the ethical implications of decisions will be presented.

Old Paradigm Systems and Ethics

Old paradigm, Eurocentric belief systems are based on assumptions developed by Bacon, Copernicus, Newton, and Descartes during the historical period known as the Enlightenment (Capra, 1982). The most significant Enlightenment beliefs are as follows (Lincoln and Guba, 1985; Harman, 1988): (1) Reality has an objective existence separate and external from the people who perceive it. (2) Objective reality can be described in a value-free manner without reference to the point of view of the observer or describer. (3) Reality can be described accurately without reference to time or context. (4) There are direct causal relationships between events. Every action can be traced to an action that preceded it. (5) Mathematics (in the form of equations) provides the most reliable map of reality, the best picture of relationships between cause and effect. (6) Universal scientific laws govern physical events, and the most satisfactory explanations of phenomena are universal explanations. In addition to these fundamental assumptions, the Enlightenment perspective also asserted that God was no longer at the center of the human experience, that it was man's (sic) role to master and subdue "nature" through scientific inquiry. Scientific, empirical knowledge was the most, possibly the only, reliable form of knowledge. Authority no longer resided in inspiration, revelation, or tradition but in empirical information (Harman, 1988).

Copernicus, Galileo, Newton, and Descartes established a radically different view of reality than the one that had dominated Christian Europe for the preceding millennium. "In 1600 an educated man (most educated persons were men) *knew* that the Earth was the center of the cosmos—the seat of change, decay, and Christian redemption. . . . A hundred years later this man's equally Christian descendant, say, his great grandson, knew . . . that the Earth was but one of many planets orbiting around one of many stars" (Harman, 1988, p. 8). Harman also points out that the changes in belief about universal authority were also changes in belief about reality in all its aspects. The first man saw the world through a *teleological* belief system that told him that the universe was alive, purposeful, and arranged by God. The second man's view was that the universe was mechanical, knowable and not mysterious, lawful, and not purposeful. God was no longer directly involved, and people were responsible for "husbanding" the earth's resources for human betterment, using science as their tool.

Ethical systems that guide human behavior are always based on fundamental assumptions about reality—the world in which people live, what elements of reality can be considered good for people and the environment, and what issues are of common concern for human welfare. "Every society ever known rests on some set of largely tacit basic assumptions abut *who we are, what kind of universe we are in and what is ultimately important to us*" (Harman, 1988, p. 10). During the Enlightenment, all the assumptions that had governed the medieval era in Europe changed. People found themselves in a new world in a new and rudderless era where their former beliefs could not guide them. As Matthew Arnold, lamenting this loss of faith, wrote in "Dover Beach" ([1867] 1962, p. 904)

The Sea of Faith
Was once too at the full and round earth's shore . . .
But now I only hear its melancholy, long withdrawing roar,

Retreating to the breath of the night wind, down the vast edges drear
And naked shingles of the world.

Enlightenment thinking dominated discussions of ethics in student affairs and in most other professions for most of the twentieth century. This means that ethical dilemmas were resolved by referring to universally accepted principles and exploring the implications of acting on those principles in a particular situation (Kitchener, 1985). *Situation Ethics,* written in 1966 by Joseph Fletcher, challenged the Enlightenment position. Fletcher caused an uproar among principle-centered thinkers who had begun to lose faith in traditional principles but were unable to provide a new ethical framework for the post-Holocaust world. Fletcher examined the catastrophic dilemmas of World War II and attempted to focus ethics on a single standard that was so general that it had to be interpreted contextually, or situationally.

The organizing construct for situation ethics was benevolence, an approach to ethical living that treats love and justice as two complementary dimensions of the broader construct. Doing good was equivalent to doing right in situation ethics. If a conflict occurred between a person's ideas about good and right, good was intended to prevail and the notion of right would be adjusted to the situation. Although Fletcher asserted that the use of one principle could guide all ethical decision making, a position that appears to reflect the Enlightenment approach, he can also be seen as the person who began to deconstruct universal-principle approaches to ethics and develop a new constructivist, contextual approach.

Situation ethics states that ethical decisions must be made about particular situations, in particular contexts. Although Fletcher did not specifically discuss the implications of cultural worldviews on ethical decision making, his discussion of a woman who had sex with a concentration camp guard in order to preserve her own life and then loved the child because it symbolized her continuing ability to live and love the rest of her family suggests the dramatic impact of circumstances on ethics. Because different cultures view the world in dramatically different ways and accept a wide range of behavior as good, it is possible to interpret Fletcher as one author who opened the door to taking both culture and context into account in ethics. In student affairs situation ethics is used whenever a conflict between rules and individual needs occurs. For example, many colleges close all residence halls for winter recess, forcing some students to return to their family's home because they have nowhere else to go. Most colleges have students from abusive families. For them, going "home" is harmful. The rules state that all students must leave the residence halls. Using a situation ethics approach, a staff member would be expected to help a student find an alternative place to stay. If the problem were widespread, situation ethics would require the development of alternative housing for students with serious need. The recess dilemma also applies to resident international students who cannot make alternative arrangements as well as students from families living in dangerous neighborhoods who do not want to go home for fear of street violence.

What is the New Paradigm? Culture, Respect, and Interaction

Whereas the old paradigm embodied universal principles, orderliness, and reversible, linear cause-and-effect relationships, the new paradigm embodies chaos, context, unpredictability and irreversibility of change. The new paradigm emphasizes the power of relationships and information in a context of nonlinear interaction. Robert Shweder, a cultural psychologist, uses the notion of *intentional worlds* to describe the different ways in which human beings from different cultures describe, engage with, and imagine their physical, emotional, and intellectual realities (Stigler, Shweder, and Herdt, 1990). "A principle of intentional worlds is that nothing real 'just is'" (p. 3). Shweder recognizes that people from the same culture tend to interpret the significance of events in roughly equivalent ways, but he does not discount the effect of individual differences on perception, interpretation, or meaning attribution. Shweder characterizes Enlightenment, or old paradigm, thinking via the twin themes of unity and uniformity: "unity in mankind's respect for the sole authority of reason, and evidence . . . ; uniformity in the substantive conclusions about how to live and what to believe . . . (normative uniformity of mankind)" (Shweder, 1984, p. 27). New paradigm thinking, in contrast, asserts that in any given ethical dilemma, multiple ethical belief systems may be operative and interactive. The resultant interpretation of events and the subsequent behavior of those involved might generate ethical chaos, a blend of interpretations in which no particular set of ideas about "the good" would dominate and no resolution or course of behavior would be taken for granted.

Examples of this phenomenon abound. What is the "right" thing for the United States to do in its dealings with countries that use prison or child labor? Is it "right" to impose U.S. standards for childhood freedom and school attendance on impoverished countries where child income is essential to family economic survival? Is it better to put prisoners on chain gangs, as we do in the United States, than to force them to produce goods for the U.S. market, as they do in China? Who is "right" in the Arab/Israeli conflict? Would a single terrorist act change ideas about right and wrong? Was Rabin's murderer right because he justified his action as an act of war and the Talmud permits assassination in time of war?

Closer to home, is it right to designate financial aid for people of color and use different standards for determining qualification or need than one might use for a white person? Can residence halls be justified as "theme houses" if the themes are African American culture or Latin American culture or Wellness? The first two themes imply different meanings than the third because of the history of African Americans and Latinos/as in the United States. Both involve ambiguous situations because an African American theme house houses African American students. The culture cannot be separated from its members.

Is a residence hall whose program emphasizes African American culture also a segregated hall, particularly if no white students choose to live in it? What standard should prevail—a student's desire to be comfortable and validated in his or her living environment or refusal to discriminate on the basis of race?

The ambiguity in these situations reflects a lack of national consensus about what is right and what is good with regard to racial issues. In the absence of consensus, ethical decision making requires extensive dialogue among the concerned groups about the nature of right and good (see Talley, this volume). Ethical and educationally sound practice on most campuses today requires open discussion of the beliefs about right and good that underlie student life policies, because many of these policies were based on the unacknowledged acceptance of principles that have not been made explicit or questioned.

Was it right for the president of a suburban university to permit five white women to move out of a residence suite because the sixth roommate was an African American who had been assigned to live with them? He posed the dilemma to the director of housing as "You can do the right thing [refuse permission to move] and have these and possibly many other white parents down on you and perhaps lose all five students, or you can do the expedient, politically less explosive thing and let them move so that the local civil rights organizations won't be having press conferences on your front lawn." The president and the director were struggling with conflicting ideas about right and good in a fast-moving, emotionally charged situation. If the white students lived in intentional worlds in which black students were seen as either the same as them or different but desirable roommates, the situation would have been framed differently. If the black student were easily frightened or desirous of avoiding conflict, the situation would have been framed differently.

Could principles guide decision making in this situation, or would the situation, with its emotionally chaotic interactions, dominate responses? Principle-oriented ethics assumes linear, cause-and-effect relationships between people and events. Situation ethics more closely resembles New Paradigm assumptions about chaotic interactions, nonlinear relationships, and unpredictable outcomes. Autonomy, faithfulness, institutional reputation, potential for student learning, parental and public oversight, the director's desire to remain employed, and the students' need to confirm their living arrangements immediately were all factors. Time was a key factor. Students and families wanted a decision in an hour or less. None of the student and family participants were willing to talk to each other. Standing on one principle, such as faithfulness to the institutional policy of nondiscrimination, might have undermined the institution's support for the principle of doing no harm, by forcing people to live together in circumstances so uncomfortable that one or more of them might have withdrawn from school. If the university were perceived as unwilling to support African American students in housing, how could the president retain credibility for his community support programs of tutoring and recreation for local children? The interaction among multiple values and priorities in the situation overpowered the administrative ability to impose a single principle on decision making.

The most effective approach would have involved a matrix in which principles such as faithfulness, justice, and autonomy were balanced against situational factors such as political realities, the intentional worlds of the students, and the ability of the institution to draw students from different racial backgrounds. This type of approach is discussed in the chapters on assessment (Banning) and management (Talley) elsewhere in this volume. It has the capacity to generate consensus about values within a particular campus community and to educate all participants about ethical thinking. Such dialogues are slow and often painful. They cannot occur in the midst of a crisis. Over the long term, however, they can turn crises into opportunities for learning and ethical decision making and to produce effective, widely supported policies that minimize future crises.

Ethical Judgment and Cognitive Complexity

Ethical judgment of the sort required by New Paradigm thinking requires a constructivist approach (Fried, 1995) and a high level of cognitive development (King and Kitchener, 1994). King and Kitchener's Reflective Judgment Model (discussed by Guthrie in this volume) documents changes in cognitive development that permit people to engage in increasingly complex thought about ethical issues and the contexts in which they occur. In the Reflective Judgment Model cognition develops from prereflective thinking in which people "do not acknowledge—or in some cases even perceive—that knowledge is uncertain" (King and Kitchener, 1994, p. 47) through quasi reflective thinking in which "some problems are ill-structured and . . . knowledge claims about them contain an element of uncertainty" (p. 58) to reflective thinking in which "knowledge is not a 'given,' but must be actively constructed and . . . claims of knowledge must be understood in relation to the context in which they were generated" (p. 66). The Reflective Judgment Model describes the cognitive processes by which individuals develop the capacity to take both context, or situation, and principle into account in ethical thinking. In *Developing Reflective Judgment* King and Kitchener describe the processes by which thinkers develop the capacity and skills to manage increasingly complex information within a reasoning system that enables judgments to be made despite the lack of certainty. They provide the conceptual framework within which principle-centered ethics can move toward a more constructivist approach that takes culture into account by describing the ways in which thinking becomes increasingly complex. In developing campus dialogues around ethical issues, the level of cognitive development among students is a key factor in their ability to participate effectively. A significant role for student development educators is assessment of cognitive development and design of appropriate challenge and support mechanisms to enhance students' cognitive development as they participate in the dialogue.

Marcia Baxter Magolda has provided another framework within which the development of increasingly complex thinking can be understood. In *Knowing and Reasoning in College* (1992) she traces cognitive development among college students, taking gender and content into account as well as cognitive structure. Her work provides a map that can be particularly helpful in understanding the cognitions associated with feminist ethics. The works of Baxter Magolda and King and Kitchener are complementary in many ways and provide two frameworks for understanding the processes of ethical development from a psychological perspective.

Principles, Virtues, and Communities

Western ethical thinking has been guided by principles or moral norms presumed to embody universally valued characteristics, such as fidelity, benevolence, nonmalificence, respect for autonomy, veracity, and justice (Meara, Schmidt, and Day, 1996). Sound ethical thinking involves applying relevant principles to a particular problem and deciding which principle takes precedence as a guide to action in that particular case. The dilemma of Heins and the Drug appearing in the work of Kohlberg (1969) is based on this system of assumptions. Although principalist approaches to ethics always involve a dialectic between a person's understanding of a principle and his or her construction of a specific ethical dilemma (Childress, 1994), the universal principal is always presumed to transcend the particulars of the situation and thus to provide a reliable guide to action. Principalism as understood in Eurocentric cultures is grounded in Enlightenment thought. However, it can operate within any cultural context, including contexts defined by gender, sexual orientation, or a corporate environment, because it elevates the principles that guide the culture. In the corporate world the dominant principle is often that of maximizing profits. In a gay or lesbian community, a major principle involves protecting people's privacy in intimate relationships. Principalism becomes difficult to use in situations in which many cultures intersect or cultures are changing so rapidly that no set of principles command universal allegiance or dominate, even within the specific setting.

Principles and the Internet. Extreme examples of the limits of principalism are illustrated by problems on the Internet. The Internet recognizes no national boundaries and has spawned hundreds of "communities of interest" around everything from recreation to politics, science, sexual practices, matters of faith, and help for students with their homework. Freedom of expression is a highly valued principle in the United States. On the Internet Americans are free to produce pornography, express beliefs about ethnic groups, support neo-Nazism, announce rallies for or against anything, and encourage lobbying and other forms of political action. Communities of interest are virtual, usually lacking a geographic or cultural base. Participants usually belong to other political, ethnic, or spiritual communities that may be guided by contradictory values. If the Arab Student Union on a campus in the United States is having a rally to protest Israeli policies or specific actions and wants to announce it on the Internet, sending that message to Arab students in Germany might pose a problem. In Germany freedom of speech and association is limited in cases considered disruptive to domestic tranquillity. If a neo-Nazi group on a U.S. campus posts an announcement to all student organizations on the Internet having "African American" or "Jewish" in their titles, its action might be considered either harassment or freedom of speech. American jurisprudence, generally guided by legal principles, cannot achieve consensus about an approach to hate crimes, including harassment, even though freedom of speech tends to dominate decisions. When communication flows freely between countries having very different legal systems and guiding principles, what is the ethical response of a university's Internet administrator who discovers a "nigger joke" Web site or a site that solicits anti-Semitic essays for worldwide distribution? Once again, this problem is most effectively viewed as an occasion for dialogue rather than one that demands a unilateral decision. Campuses have developed committees whose major purpose is the discussion of these kinds of ethical dilemmas, and the Internet itself is home to numerous discussion sites for exchanging information between campuses.

Principles in Scholarship. In classrooms on campuses in the United States, ethical dilemmas abound when principalism is the dominant approach. A professor of anthropology in a secular university has reported great difficulty in communicating with a Muslim graduate student trained as an undergraduate to interpret all his data through the principles of the Koran (Gailey, in conversation). In the United States, comments from religious texts may be used to support an argument, but they are never used as the sole justification in an academic paper written in a secular college or university. Most Islamic states are theocracies. Separation of church and state is not only unfamiliar to a Muslim student but can easily be seen as a desecration. Which set of principles dominates in this dilemma—the student's faith or the institution's standards for academic work? What status does the principle of freedom of religion hold in this argument? Making decisions about conflicting principles becomes more difficult as authority claims become more absolute.

Universities and colleges have become multicultural organizations because of the many communities in which students, faculty, and staff participate, virtual, ethnic, and other. Each community may have its own set of guiding principles. Each person tends to emerge from several communities, and there is no reliable way to predict which set of principles will dominate at any specific time, in any specific situation. With regard to academic processes and student behavior, a university has the right to pronounce its own principles and to inform students before they matriculate (freedom of information, informed consent), but the administration and faculty cannot predict the relative strength of any specific principle in any specific situation. Two other approaches have recently emerged that can contribute to a matrix that includes context, constructs, principles, and virtues.

Virtue Ethics. Virtue ethics shifts the focus from principles to characteristics of particular people in particular contexts. Virtues or traits are considered to be personal qualities that are deemed meritorious in a particular context. Beauchamp and Childress state that "a virtue is a trait of character that is socially valued and a *moral virtue* is a trait that is morally valued" (Beauchamp and Childress, 1994; cited in Meara, Schmidt, and Day, 1996, p. 24). Virtue ethics provides a more complete picture of the relationship between moral reasoning and moral action. In principle-centered ethics, a person can easily know what he or she ought to do, based on principled reasoning, and still be unable or unwilling to do it. In contrast, "Proponents of virtue ethics believe that motivation, emotion, character, ideals and moral habits situated within the traditions and practices of a culture or other group present a more complete account of the moral life than actions based on prescribed rules" (Meara, Schmidt, and Day, 1996, p. 24).

Virtue ethics is based on ideals of human behavior in particular contexts. Virtue ethics can evolve as new communities evolve. For example, a group of recent graduates of a college student development Master's degree program decided to establish a listserv in order to stay in touch and provide support and consultation for each other. One of the first topics on the list was ethics in the interviewing process. The conversation moved from abstract, "what if" sorts of questions to questions about responses to inappropriate behavior to repetitive complaining with requests for sympathy, but no effort was made to evaluate situations. The next stage in the conversation began when one member raised the issue of conversational content and the ethics of quasi-public professional discussion. The members of this virtual community have begun to set ideals for their listserv community, and their set of virtues will emerge through dialogue.

Meara, Schmidt, and Day (1996) suggest that virtues are community specific and culturally and situationally defined. The virtues they consider most significant in the community of counseling psychologists are *prudence, integrity, respectfulness, and benevolence*. Virtue ethics focuses on ideal behavior and relies on the character and judgment of the agent in addressing particular problems in specific contexts. Every campus is free to construct and publicize its own set of virtues and to use them in setting standards for ethical behavior. Ideas about virtue may vary among campuses because of different campus missions and cultures. Thus a person's virtuous behavior in a particular situation can be more flexible than the behavior of a person who makes principle-centered decisions. Because a great deal of student affairs practice is devoted to helping students, the thinking of counseling psychologists in the domain of ethics transfers well to the student affairs profession.

Student affairs professionals are often faced with dilemmas resulting from the intersection of many value systems in one location. A classic example is the difference in the timing of parties held by African American students and white students. Typically African American student parties begin much later than parties organized by white students and end later as well. If the desired or only available location for a party is in the basement of a residence hall, whose needs and desires prevail—the students who want to party until three in the morning or the students who want to sleep at that time? A student affairs specialist approaching this dilemma from a virtue ethics perspective would be free to discuss the problems with each group, determine the meaning of the activities for each group, and try to create a solution respecting the belief systems, common social behaviors, and values of both groups, with or without an intergroup meeting. Prudence, benevolence, integrity, and respectfulness would all come into play.

A student affairs staff person using principle-centered ethics would be far more constrained in addressing this problem. How does one decide what is fair when both groups want to use the same space to conduct incompatible activities? What is justice when the rules for use of space and time restrictions were decided by an overwhelmingly white administration in ignorance of many social practices of African American students? This is an old problem that has generally been solved by designating nonresidential spaces for late-night parties. When the problem first arose in the 1970s, it was perceived by many white administrators as a case of African American students trying to break the rules. The basis on which the rules had been established, common (white) assumptions about when to sleep and when to socialize, were not easily challenged. They were perceived as commonsensical, not to be broken. Many campuses have come a long way since that time, but there are more current problems that illustrate the same "principles versus virtues" dilemma. Two of these dilemmas are acquaintance rape versus rough sex and harassment versus freedom of expression.

Acquaintance Rape or Rough Sex? Campus administrations have tended to address acquaintance rape by attempting to define it and responding to allegations according to rules and principles in a conduct code. Acquaintance rape is said to have happened when two people know each other, one of them does not consent to sexual intercourse with the other, and the other persists to consummation. Any person who has been sexually active or who has seen any R-rated movies understands that rules may be written about acquaintance rape but they do not begin to cover the complexities of sexual interaction. Decisions are made second by second. What would a prudent person do in a sexual encounter? What would a person of integrity do? A prudent person would probably think far in advance about the level of sexual involvement she or he wants, the dangers involved, the level of trust in the relationship, and personal responsibility. A person of integrity would probably find ways to express in advance what she or he expects or intends. A person who behaves respectfully and benevolently would listen to his or her partner and respect the partner's wishes even if they conflicted with her or his desires. At the moment before intercourse, which is likely to most influence the decision to consummate—principles and rules, or character?

The situation is complex, fast-paced and nonrational even when both persons are from the same culture and are following the same assumptions about sexual behavior. On modern American campuses students often date across racial and ethnic lines. Many students experiment with homosexual as well as heterosexual relationships. A student who is sure about his homosexual identity will tend to have clearer ideas about what will happen on a date than a man who is unsure about his sexual identity. What does consent mean for a young man who is experimenting with sexual behavior if, after the encounter begins, he becomes quite sure that he does not want to continue? He began by consenting, and he changed his mind. Is there any guarantee that the more experienced partner will pay careful attention to the resistance expressed or will respect a request to stop? The same set of circumstances and problems could be raised between a man and woman, either of whom came from a culture that expected virginity before marriage. For a student far from home, excited by the freedom on American campuses and inexperienced, when is a yes a no? When is a no a yes? How does early socialization, particularly for women who are trained to defer to men, work in this situation?

Michael Rion (1989) has suggested a set of questions that individual practitioners can ask about ethically disturbing situations to clarify their thinking and plan action. If a worried student consults a student affairs professional the day after an incident of nonconsensual or upsetting sex, the following questions might be discussed.

Why is this incident bothering the student? Does the student believe that she or he imposed her or his will on somebody else or submitted to an imposition? Did the student violate some previously held beliefs without rethinking the beliefs? Did the behavior seem "right" yesterday and "wrong" today? Did the student do harm to the partner or permit the partner to do harm to him or her? Was the issue alcohol consumption rather than sexual engagement? Is the student upset that she or he did not actually make a decision but just let things happen? Helping students clarify their own thinking and inherent beliefs about nonmarital sex begins the action-reflection cycle that leads to increased self-understanding and self-direction.

Who else matters? Does the student need to discuss this with last night's partner, a roommate, a member of the clergy, parents? Is there anyone else who needs to know or has a right to know?

Is it my problem? Does the student have to settle this distress in his or her own mind, apologize to the partner, or discuss her or his drinking patterns with an alcohol counselor? Is the student interested in bringing the problem to the campus judicial officer? Where does the student's responsibility lie in addressing this problem?

What is the ethical concern? This question is the core of the ethical education process in this situation. What are the student's principles, values, and beliefs about good character? The role of a student affairs professional at this point is that of counselor.

What do (significant) others think? After the student has been helped to clarify his or her own thinking, it might be useful or comforting for the student to consider the opinions that significant others hold about nonconsensual or upsetting sex. Would friends advise prosecution, mediation, apology, or counseling? Taking conflicting opinions held by trusted peers into account is an important way of gaining perspective on one's own ideas.

Am I being true to myself? After all the thinking, reflecting, and evaluating, does the student feel as if the resolution "fits" with his or her character? Does she or he believe that they will be able to avoid this type of situation in the future? Is the resolution satisfying, even if last night's behavior was not?

By engaging with a student in a dialogue guided by Rion's questions, the student affairs staff member can support the student without having to decide what "really" happened or if it "really" was a rape. This process leads the student through a thinking/feeling process that brings him or her to increased awareness of his or her ideas about personal ethics, community ethics, principles, and virtues in an atmosphere of respect and acceptance. Although campuses must have rules and opportunities for the redress of injustice in order to ensure fairness and protect student welfare, the rules have limited effectiveness in this situation if the student does not understand his or her own behavior and beliefs. A counselor can focus on virtues, whereas a judicial officer must consider rules and principles. When both approaches are used, the outcome is likely to be more educationally sound than if one were used to the exclusion of the other.

Freedom of Speech or Harassment? A similarly complex problem is that of harassment: racial, sexual, ethnic, electronic, or face-to-face. Freedom of speech is one of the most basic principles in American culture and is absolutely fundamental to campus discourse. Freedom of speech has presented an intractable ethical dilemma for administrators, and, to date, no regulations designed to limit this principle have survived legal challenges. In face-to-face conversation the willingness of most people to be rude and abusive is limited by the potential consequences—receiving equal doses of rudeness and abuse from the other person. Limits on abusive, face-to-face interactions arise from one's reading of nonverbal cues, assessment of potential physical threats, and willingness and ability to respond in kind as well as one's moral upbringing regarding whether fights are virtuous or shameful. In some tribal cultures an insult to one member of the family is considered an insult to the whole family and demands a comparable response in order to maintain family honor. As in a sexual encounter, decisions about advancing toward engagement are made on a second-by-second basis and judgments can change in an instant. Such limits seem not to apply in instances of "flaming" on the Internet, in which the level of verbal abuse, character assassination, and threats to safety have escalated in recent years. Can a principled approach to ethics and student behavior provide an effective guide if an aggressor does not acknowledge the validity of rules and can violate them in anonymity for a long time?

Many cases of harassment fall outside the rules because they involve behavior that was impossible before the development of the Internet. In one case a male student wrote a computer program that automatically kept track of a female student's whereabouts by recording where she logged on (Richardson, personal communication). He could have stalked her, if he wished to do so, through his electronic tracking system. Technically, the student did not violate the judicial code because he had not physically stalked the woman, but he had created an atmosphere of intimidation that was harmful in itself. When an administrator is aware of a potentially harmful situation, there is an ethical obligation to consider taking action. This type of situation raises both ethical and judicial questions for student affairs administrators. Ethical guidelines must be used to address two questions: Should the administrator respond to the situation, and if so, what is the ethical response? Is there an ethical imperative to raise policy questions so that additional instances of this type of behavior will fall within the boundaries of existing policy? Ethical questions tend to precede policy questions in uncharted territory such as this. Policy and judicial codes should be based on clearly stated ethical principles and virtues shared by the community for which they are written. Robert Greenleaf suggests an approach to ethical thinking and action in his work on servant leadership in higher education (1991). Servant leaders are always searching and listening. They are "affirmative builders of a better society" (p. 12) who consistently ask about the effects of their choices on the most privileged and the least privileged members of their community and always ask themselves "What are you trying to do?" (p. 15) before taking action. Servant leadership provides a process model that takes both principles and virtues into account.

Principles and Virtues in the Human Community

On the multicultural campuses of the twenty-first century, no single system of ethical beliefs and practices can or should prevail. The Enlightenment system that has dominated Eurocentric cultures violates or ignores significant elements of ethical systems that dominate in other parts of the world. For example, most Islamic countries are theocracies. Government policies are heavily influenced by Islamic law. Democracies are generally secular and support freedom of religion as well as freedom from religious intrusion in personal life. In a democracy, no person is entitled to political leadership by virtue of his or her ordination or affirmation of faith. People from these two different kinds of cultures have dramatically different ideas about the source or sources of authority in public and private life and about the degree of submission to authority that is expected or can be tolerated. On campuses where Muslims from the Middle East and Christians and Jews from Europe and North America live and study together, the ethical practices of the student affairs staff must take all these variables into account.

There is no single set of principles by which ethical decisions can be made when providing student services to students from a wide range of backgrounds. The virtues suggested by Meara, Schmidt, and Day (1996) provide some guidance—benevolence, respect, prudence and integrity—but these virtues must be used in the context of the principles that govern campus decision making and student conduct. Because every campus can be considered a culture within which several subcultures coexist (Kuh, 1993; Person, 1995), student affairs professionals should address ethical issues as part of all policy discussions. Even operational decisions tend to require a brief examination of ethical implications. A critical element in this process is that of mindfulness, or "mutual co-arising": the notion that everything is connected to everything else and nothing can be taken for granted (Hanh, 1987). No single set of principles or beliefs can be assumed to dominate, but all relevant beliefs must be examined for their potential impact on everyone involved. Because of different belief systems and different ways of interpreting events, the consequences of a particular choice can easily move in unanticipated directions because different groups interpret the meaning of events differently and those interpretations may not be known to the decision makers. Student affairs administrators who previously believed that they had a reasonably accurate sense of the ways students would react to decisions, use services, or participate in programs can no longer have the luxury of these beliefs until they have thoroughly reviewed them.

The student affairs profession has evolved in a historical and cultural context that rests on particular assumptions about behavior, values, language, and cognitive categories (Fried, 1995). Student affairs as a profession is practically unique to the United States and is often culturally encapsulated. This profession has been responsible for managing student behavior according to the prevailing codes of the culture and the community. These codes are heavily influenced by the dominant national values. Finally, student affairs operates within the prescribed cognitive categories of U.S. higher education, which tends to separate living from learning, thinking from feeling, spirituality from secular life, teaching from learning, and knowledge from action (Fried, 1995). As a consequence of the cultural encapsulation of student affairs, it might be suggested that this profession has a long road to walk in moving toward a multicultural approach to ethics.

As a profession, we must challenge our own complacency about the ethical principles that have served us in dealing with a more homogeneous student community and begin to examine the multiple value and belief systems on which our current students are basing their lives (Hughes, 1992). Most colleges and universities in the United States are no longer completely of the United States, as it has been historically represented. Immigrants, refugees, international students, native people, Latinos, African Americans, Asian Americans, gays, lesbians, bisexuals, and people with disabilities populate our campuses and expect their beliefs and behaviors to be respected. Members of each group have slightly different needs, priorities, and expectations about college attendance. Not to attend to this vast range of expectations and priorities is to violate both ethical principles and virtues. To ignore the different beliefs about goodness and virtue held by different groups of students is to ignore the other-regarding virtues of benevolence and integrity and the principles of autonomy, justice, fairness, doing good, and doing no harm. This violates the historical belief system of student affairs and fails to honor the historical mission of providing service to students as individuals and members of groups.

Hughes (1992, pp. 210–211) has discovered several universal human values that are interpreted differently from culture to culture but can provide some new and transcendent organizing constructs for the creation of a multicultural ethical process for student affairs. In summary, the values are as follows:

Personal development through spiritual freedom, educational opportunity, and wellness
Human rights and dignity through respect for cultural and individual identity
Collaborative, peaceful approaches to conflict resolution and management
Development of global ethical codes to enhance the quality of human life

Although all people develop their ethical beliefs within a particular cultural milieu, these beliefs do not remain static. They evolve as individuals face situations for which their previous ethical beliefs have not prepared them. These situations arise with increasing frequency as individuals move out into a world where members of different cultural groups interact constantly. Ethical decision making now requires an active inquiry process in which virtues, principles, community expectations, and standards are all examined as choices are made. For student affairs professionals, the dynamic of ethical inquiry suggests two major components: attending to our own ethical assumptions and reexamining them in the light of our student populations, the ways we serve them, and the manner in which we conduct ourselves; and identifying situations in which we can contribute to the ethical education of students who will live their lives in multicultural communities of all sorts—virtual, residential, professional, and spiritual.

Conclusion

Our own professional development and the ethical education of students can be addressed with a combination of Hanh's mindfulness and Hughes's challenge to complacency. Ironically, Aristotle, one of the earliest Western ethicists, provides the framework within which we can move toward these goals. Aristotle believed that the purpose of ethical inquiry was to determine "the good" in both the universal and the particular. He also believed that the public good set the context for individual virtues, intellectual concerns, and practical occupations. In modern terminology, individual welfare had to be examined in the total context of community welfare, and examining one without the other was considered meaningless (McKeon, 1941). In order to challenge complacency and practice mindfulness with students, student affairs professionals can take no outcome for granted and must raise questions when students fail to consider the ethical implications of the choices they make. This approach requires a transcendence of the historical categories of analysis. Asking students what they consider good in a situation slows down the decision-making process, may possibly generate anger or resistance, and forces all participants to examine their basic assumptions before proceeding. Intellect and emotions become involved. Student affairs professionals must be able to reflect student feelings and beliefs and at the same time provide information about ethical decision making and various ethical systems. They must identify issues, challenge and support students, keep the welfare of the individuals and the institution in mind, and reexamine what *good* means in the specific situation. Helping students learn how to think about ethics becomes far more important than helping them make the "right" choice. Notions of right, goodness, and justice vary by culture and need to be understood in the context of campus cultures, national culture, and a variety of other cultures. Guthrie, in this volume, describes the levels of cognitive complexity that are necessary for sound ethical thinking. Her analysis applies to student affairs professionals as well as to students. Taking cultural information, context, virtues, and principles into account is an extremely demanding task. Professional responsibility and competence is the first standard in the "Statement of Ethical Principles and Standards" of the American College Personnel Association (1993). On multicultural campuses, our most demanding professional code of ethics requires that we undertake the task in order to remain competent and responsible.

References

American College Personnel Association, Standing Committee on Ethics. "A Statement of Ethical Principles and Standards." *Journal of College Student Development,* 1993, *34,* 89–92.

Arnold, M. "Dover Beach." In M. Abrams (ed.), *The Norton Anthology of English Literature.* Vol. 2. New York: W. W. Norton, 1962. (Originally published 1867.)

Baxter Magolda, M. B. *Knowing and Reasoning in College: Gender-Related Patterns in Students' Intellectual Development.* San Francisco: Jossey-Bass, 1992.

Capra, F. *The Turning Point: Science, Society and the Rising of Culture.* New York: Simon and Schuster, 1982.

Childress, J. "Principles Oriented Bioethics." In E. DuBose, R. Hamel, and L. O'Connell (eds). *A Matter of Principles? Ferment in Bioethics.* Valley Forge, Pa.: Trinity International Press, 1994.

Fletcher, J. *Situation Ethics.* Philadelphia, Pa.: Westminster Press, 1966.

Fried, J. *Shifting Paradigms in Student Affairs.* Washington, D.C.: American College Personnel Association, 1995.

Geertz, C. *Local Knowledge.* New York: Basic Books, 1983.

Greenleaf, R. *Servant Leadership.* New York: Paulist Press, 1991.

Hanh, T. N. *Interbeing.* Berkeley, Calif.: Paralax Press, 1987.

Harman, W. *Global Mind Change.* New York: Warner Books, 1988.

Hughes, M. "Global Diversity and Student Development: Educating for World Citizenship." In M. Terrell (ed.), *Diversity, Disunity and Campus Community.* Washington, D.C.: National Association of Student Personnel Administrators, 1992.

King, P. M., and Kitchener, K. S. *Developing Reflective Judgment: Understanding and Promoting Intellectual Growth and Critical Thinking in Adolescents and Adults.* San Francisco: Jossey-Bass, 1994.

Kitchener, K. "Ethical Principles and Ethical Decisions in Student Affairs." In H. J. Canon and R. D. Brown (eds.), *Applied Ethics in Student Services.* New Directions for Student Services, no. 30. San Francisco: Jossey-Bass, 1985.

Kohlberg, L. "Stage and Sequence: The Cognitive Developmental Approach to Socialization." In D. A. Goslin (ed.), *Handbook of Socialization Theory and Research.* Skokie, Ill.: Rand McNally, 1969.

Kuh, G. (ed.). *Cultural Perspectives in Student Affairs Work.* Washington, D.C.: American College Personnel Association, 1993.

Lincoln, Y., and Guba, E. *Naturalistic Inquiry*. Newbury Park, Calif.: Sage, 1985.

McKeon, R. (ed). *The Basic Works of Aristotle*. New York: Random House, 1941.

Meara, N., Schmidt, L., and Day, J. "Principles and Virtues: A Foundation for Ethical Decisions, Policies and Character." *Counseling Psychologist,* 1996, *24,* 4–77.

Person, D. "Students of Color and Student Culture." In J. Fried and Associates (eds.), *Shifting Paradigms in Student Affairs*. Washington, D.C.: American College Personnel Association, 1995.

Rion, M. *The Responsible Manager*. Amherst, Mass.: HRD Press, 1989.

Shweder, R. "Anthropology's Romantic Rebellion Against the Enlightenment, or There's More to Thinking Than Reason and Evidence." In R. Shweder and R. LeVine (eds.), *Culture Theory*. Cambridge, U.K.: Cambridge University Press, 1984.

Stigler, J., Shweder, R., and Herdt, G. *Cultural Psychology*. New York: Cambridge University Press, 1990.

JANE FRIED is associate professor in the Department of Health and Human Services at Central Connecticut State University and is former chair of the Standing Committee on Ethics of the American College Personnel Association.

This chapter presents the basics of intellectual development necessary
for comprehension of the ethical development of college students and a
model on which interventions can be built.

Cognitive Foundations of Ethical Development

Victoria L. Guthrie

> It's hard for me. I know that I shouldn't think bad about them, but
> I've had bad experiences and it's hard not to stereotype all of
> them. . . . I try not to be prejudiced, but it's hard when you've had
> a bad experience with someone. It plays on the rest of your life.
> —Leah, freshman

> Just being on a college campus where you have tons of different
> people, different kinds of people, you know, different racial back-
> grounds and all that stuff . . . So now, coming to college, it's like—
> I mean I knew they were out there and stuff—I guess I'm more
> aware of the different types of people.
> —Lori, freshman

> Being intolerant is just being ignorant, because you're not seeing
> what's out there.
> —Donald, junior

> I think being more tolerant is more challenging. It makes you think
> more. It's harder. It's easier to be intolerant.
> —Stuart, doctoral student

Each of these students is struggling with one of college's most challenging ethical and moral dilemmas: dealing with the great diversity of people, cultures,
beliefs, and behaviors daily encountered on campus. The ability to respect

23

human differences and to deal effectively with different individuals has become integral to the mission of higher education. For example, the statement, "Wisdom, sound judgment, tolerance and respect for other persons, cultures, and ideas are the hallmarks of an educated person and the characteristics that the University hopes to develop in its students," found in the Bowling Green State University 1993–1995 undergraduate catalog (p. 3), represents a common goal espoused in college and university mission statements.

Tolerance for increasing diversity in today's complex and global society is a significant challenge for most college students. In addition to perennial ethical dilemmas within the academy, such as those involving academic integrity, students in this era have to deal with previously unimagined ethical issues. Civility in cyberspace and sexuality in the era of AIDS are just two examples. How do students learn to weigh the issues involved and come to an ethical stance of their own? What should the role of higher education be in this process? How do educators assist students in their development of these abilities? What specific models and theories provide guidance for interventions to challenge and support ethical development during the college years? These questions form the basis of this chapter on the cognitive foundations of ethical development. Because the development of tolerance or respect for human diversity is such a powerful example, it will be used as a central conceptual basis for this chapter. A framework having applications for a wide range of ethical issues will be built around it.

This chapter combines theories of intellectual and moral development with an examination of the underlying cognitive structures and abilities necessary for ethical decision making. It then presents a model on which interventions can be built. King and Kitchener's (1994) Reflective Judgment Model is used in the discussion of the relationship between intellectual development and ethical judgment. Rest's (1984) four-component model of morality is then presented as a guide for specific interventions with college students.

Higher Education and Character Development

Since the founding of the first colonial colleges in America, the development of the student's character has been among the goals of higher education (Brubacher and Rudy, 1976). The religious and moral development of students was initially the primary function of higher education; in America's first institutions of higher education, "moral development goals were professed openly and unashamedly" (Brown and Canon, 1978, p. 427). However, with the creation of state (secular) institutions through the Land Grant Act of 1862 came "ever-increasing concern for the separation of church and state and less concern with religious and moral development" (p. 427). In addition, the early twentieth-century movement to emulate the German tradition of higher education by elevating objectivity and the scientific method in a rationalistic philosophy established "the principal role of higher education [to be] intellectual and not moral" (Brubacher and Rudy, 1976, p. 296). When American higher education began to adopt a university model emphasizing research and scholarship, faculty assumed a stance of ethical neutrality and shed their old college responsibility for the value development of students (Sandeen, 1985). This philosophy of academic objectivity reached a point in the 1960s where the university's adopted neutral or "value-free" stance stood in great contrast to the deeply-held values and moral outrage of the student protesters. "A laissez faire approach [became] the new morality" (Brown and Canon, 1978), and intentional moral development efforts were almost completely abandoned.

There has recently been a resurgence of interest in ethics and moral development in the college years. Derek Bok, former president of Harvard University, has asserted that a primary obligation of higher education is "helping students understand how to lead ethical, reflective, fulfilling lives" (1988, p. 50). He further holds that moral issues offer an opportunity for learning because they present puzzling and ambiguous problems that create educational dialogue.

> Although moral issues sometimes lack convincing answers, that is not necessarily the case. Besides, universities should be the last institutions to discourage a belief in the value of reasoned argument and carefully considered evidence in analyzing even the hardest human problems. And universities should be among the first to affirm the importance of basic norms such as honesty, promise-keeping, free expression, and helping others, for these are not only principles essential to civilized society; they are values on which all learning and discovery ultimately depend. There is nothing odd or inappropriate, therefore, for a university to use them as the foundation for a determined program to help students develop a strong set of moral standards. (Bok, 1990, p. 100)

The student affairs profession, born "primarily as a result of a shift of emphasis in education values" (Sandeen, 1985, p. 13), has from the beginning "represented an institutional attempt to retain at least a modicum of commitment to the development of human beings at a time when academic and intellectual values had come to dominate the scene" (p. 13).

Although today higher education is "still dominated by the overwhelming emphasis of the institution upon academic and vocational values" (Sandeen, 1985, p. 13), many mission statements contain specific references to the development of students' character, integrity, morality, or ethics. For example, the Oberlin College Statement of Goals and Objectives states that among that university's aims for its students is "to expand their social awareness, social responsibility, and capacity for moral judgment so as to prepare them for intelligent and useful response to the present and future demands of society" (1992, p. 1). Bowling Green State University also includes among its academic goals that of "providing quality academic programs in a learning environment that promotes academic and personal excellence in students, as well as appreciation of intellectual, ethical, and aesthetic values" (p. 3). Many significant advances in assisting students with their ethical and moral development have been made in the past twenty years (Sandeen, 1985). During the 1980s many other professions have also "rediscovered" ethics (Welfel, 1990, p. 196). Colleges and universities now have the philosophical motivation, the public support, and the theoretical tools to work toward the goal of character development.

Tolerance for Diversity: An Ethical Dilemma

Keeping in mind this historical overview of higher education's involvement in the moral and ethical development of its students, let us examine tolerance for diversity as an exemplar of the ethical dilemmas facing today's college students and explore its theoretical foundations. The development of tolerance, appreciation, and respect for human differences is a challenge immediately faced by students who, coming to college or university, discover a wide variety of people different from themselves. These differences may be in gender, race, religion, nationality, or sexual orientation, or attitude, viewpoint, belief, or perspective. The students probably face a more diverse environment than they have previously encountered on a daily basis. Dealing with this diversity requires acceptance and appreciation of differences, empathy, tolerance, and the ability to suspend judgment and try to understand different, possibly unsettling, ways of thinking and acting (Chickering and Reisser, 1993). Ethical thinking allows us to address these "troubling questions concerning our relations with other human beings" (Garrison and Rud, 1995, p. 7).

Tolerance of individual differences is a concept that draws from the fields of moral and intellectual development. Guthrie's research (1996) on tolerance for diversity among college students suggests that tolerance requires a base level of intellectual development, specifically, reflective judgment ability. Therefore, to understand college students' development of tolerance in particular, and their ethical development in general, it is necessary to first understand how intellectual and moral development interrelate.

Intellectual Development as a Precursor to Moral Development

Moral and intellectual development are related domains (Colby and Kohlberg, 1989; King and Kitchener, 1994; King, Kitchener, and Wood, 1985; King, Kitchener, Wood, and Davison, 1989; Kohlberg, 1984; Rest, 1988) that share a structural similarity (Kitchener, 1982; Kohlberg, 1981). Although the development of moral thinking and that of reflective thinking may follow similar pathways, the experiences that affect each progression may vary (Rest, Bebeau, and Volker, 1986). Moral and intellectual development both involve reasoning about ill-structured problems. Ill-structured problems in the moral domain concern making decisions about social values, especially with "how humans ought to act in particular situations or in relationship to each other in order to further human welfare" (King and Kitchener, 1994, p. 206). Decisions in the intellectual domain focus on issues of epistemology and sound reasoning in circumstances of uncertainty. Two questions arise: How do we know what we know?

What types of decisions are defensible in light of intellectual uncertainty? Therefore, whereas moral dilemmas often involve differing values or differing conceptions of the good, intellectual problems are defined here as involving epistemological issues. Both domains require the individual decision maker to base a judgment on incomplete or conflicting information or perspectives.

Research indicates that intellectual development is a necessary but not sufficient precursor to moral development. A certain level of cognitive complexity is required in order to make complex moral decisions. As King and Kitchener have suggested, "Before educators can help students learn to think more complexly about moral or identity problems, they may need to help students master the skills associated with complex thinking (or reflective thinking) itself so that they will have more complex thinking categories available to them" (1994, p. 221). The relationships between intellectual and moral development are complex; the two domains are interrelated, and development in each domain may depend on different kinds of experiences (Colby and Kohlberg, 1989; King and Kitchener, 1994). An understanding of the basics of intellectual development is necessary for comprehension of the ethical development of college students.

Cognitive-developmental theories describe the increasing degrees of complexity with which individuals make meaning of their experience. These theories are built on the work of Jean Piaget (1932) and Lawrence Kohlberg (1969, 1984). The cognitive structures are described as "stages," each of which "typically refers to a set of interrelated assumptions (about knowledge, morality, self, etc.) that give individuals a foundation from which to interpret their experiences" (King, 1990, p. 83). Several theories are specifically adult- or college-student-based, including those of Perry (1970), Belenky, Clinchy, Goldberger, and Tarule (1986), Baxter Magolda (1992), and King and Kitchener (1994). The Reflective Judgment Model (King and Kitchener, 1994; Kitchener and King, 1981) is the best known and most extensively studied (Pascarella and Terenzini, 1991). Although each of these theories is useful in understanding cognitive development, the reflective judgment approach of King and Kitchener will be used in this chapter to explicate the cognitive basis for moral development.

Intellectual Development: A Foundational Ability

King and Kitchener's Reflective Judgment Model (1994) presents a scheme in which "reasoning is seen as developing along a multilevel continuum" (Pascarella and Terenzini, 1991, p. 123) from late childhood through adulthood. Reflective judgments are defensible judgments about complex and controversial problems. People begin with an awareness of uncertainty and advance toward "integrating and evaluating data, relating those data to theory and well informed opinions, and ultimately creating a solution to the problem that can be defended as reasonable and plausible" (King and Kitchener, 1994, p. xvi). Reflective judgment is the outcome of this developmental progression.

The definition of reflective judgment is consistent with, yet distinct from, other definitions of critical thinking. It focuses on thinking about ill-structured problems—problems that "cannot be described with a high degree of completeness or solved with a high degree of certainty; in fact, it is sometimes difficult to determine when a solution has been reached" (King and Kitchener, 1994, p. 10). "What sets the Reflective Judgment Model apart from other comparable models are the observations that epistemic assumptions affect the way individuals resolve ill-structured problems and that true reflective thinking occurs only when people are engaged in thinking about problems that involve real uncertainty" (p. 41).

The Reflective Judgment Model describes a developmental progression in reasoning that utilizes seven distinct sets of assumptions, called stages, about knowledge, how knowledge is acquired, and how people justify their knowledge claims and beliefs. Each set of assumptions "has its own logical coherency" (King and Kitchener, 1994, p. 13). The stage of assumptions about reality and knowledge are used by the individual "to perceive and organize available information and to make judgments about an issue. The process of forming judgments becomes increasingly complex, sophisticated, and comprehensive from lower to higher stages" (Kitchener and King, 1981, p. 92). According to the model, individuals develop an increasingly complex ability "to evaluate knowledge claims and to explain and defend their points of view on controversial issues" (King and Kitchener, 1994, p. 13). The authors have grouped the stages into three levels of reasoning: pre-reflective, quasi-reflective, and reflective. Undergraduate college students typically use reasoning characterized as pre-reflective or quasi-reflective. The progression of thinking described by the stages of the reflective judgment model is presented in Table 2.1. Each of the three levels is briefly summarized in the following discussion.

Pre-reflective thinkers (stages 1, 2, and 3) reason on the assumption that "knowledge is gained either by direct, personal observation or through the word of an authority figure; they assume that knowledge thus gained is absolutely correct and certain" (King and Kitchener, 1994, p. 16). Well- and ill-structured problems are not differentiated. Evidence is not used to reason to a conclusion.

Reasoning at the middle stages (stages 4 and 5) "recognizes that knowledge claims about ill-structured problems contain elements of uncertainty; thus there is an understanding that some situations are truly problematic. The difficulty is in understanding how judgments ought to be made in light of this uncertainty" (King and Kitchener, 1994, p. 16). Although individuals who hold the assumptions of stages 4 or 5 may agree that judgments ought to be based on evidence, they typically consider evaluation to be individualistic and idiosyncratic. Differences between well- and ill-structured problems are admitted but are seen as problematic because of the individual's inability to deal with the ambiguity inherent in ill-structured problems.

Table 2.1. Summary of Reflective Judgment Studies

Pre-Reflective Thinking (Stages 1, 2, and 3)

Stage 1

View of knowledge: Knowledge is assumed to exist absolutely and concretely; it is not understood as an abstraction. It can be obtained with certainty by direct observation. *Concept of justification:* Beliefs need no justification since there is assumed to be an absolute correspondence between what is believed to be true and what is true. Alternate beliefs are not perceived.

"I know what I have seen."

Stage 2

View of knowledge: Knowledge is assumed to be absolutely certain or certain but not immediately available. Knowledge can be obtained directly through the senses (as in direct observation) or via authority figures. *Concept of justification:* Beliefs are unexamined and unjustified by their correspondence with the beliefs of an authority figure (such as a teacher or parent). Most issues are assumed to have a right answer, so there is little or no conflict in making decisions about disputed issues.

"If it is on the news, it has to be true."

Stage 3

View of knowledge: Knowledge is assumed to be absolutely certain or temporarily uncertain. In areas of temporary uncertainty, only personal beliefs can be known until absolute knowledge is obtained. In areas of absolute certainty, knowledge is obtained from authorities. *Concept of justification:* In areas in which certain answers exist, beliefs are justified by reference to authorities' views. In areas in which answers do not exist, beliefs are defended as personal opinion since the link between evidence and beliefs is unclear.

*"When there is evidence that people can give to convince everybody
one way or another, then it will be knowledge; until then, it's just a guess."*

Quasi-Reflective Thinking (Stages 4 and 5)

Stage 4

View of knowledge: Knowledge is uncertain and knowledge claims are idiosyncratic to the individual since situational variables (such as incorrect reporting of data, data lost over time, or disparities on access to information) dictate that knowing always involves an element of ambiguity. *Concept of justification:* Beliefs are justified by giving reasons and using evidence, but the arguments and choice of evidence are idiosyncratic (for example, choosing evidence that fits an established belief).

*"I'd be more inclined to believe evolution if they had proof. It's just like the pyramids:
I don't think we'll ever know. Who are you going to ask? No one was there."*

Stage 5

View of knowledge: Knowledge is contextual and subjective since it is filtered through a person's perceptions and criteria for judgment. Only interpretations of evidence, events, or issues may be known. *Concept of justification:* Beliefs are justified within a particular context by means of the rules of inquiry for that context and by context-specific interpretations of evidence. Specific beliefs are assumed to be context specific or are balanced against other interpretations, which complicates (and sometimes delays) conclusions.

*"People think differently and so they attack the problem differently.
Other theories could be as true as my own, but based on different evidence."*

Table 2.1, (cont.)

Reflective Thinking (Stages 6 and 7)

Stage 6
View of knowledge: Knowledge is constructed into conclusions about ill-structured problems on the basis of information from a variety of sources. Interpretations that are based on evaluations of evidence across contexts and on the evaluated opinions of reputable others can be known.
Concept of justification: Beliefs are justified by comparing evidence and opinion from different perspectives on an issue or across different contexts and by constructing solutions that are evaluated by criteria such as the weight of the evidence, the utility of the solution, or the pragmatic need for action.

"It's very difficult in this life to be sure. There are degrees of sureness.
You come to a point at which you are sure enough for a personal stance on the issue."

Stage 7
View of knowledge: Knowledge is the outcome of a process of reasonable inquiry in which solutions to ill-structured problems are constructed. The adequacy of those solutions is evaluated in terms of what is most reasonable or probable according to the current evidence, and it is reevaluated when relevant new evidence, perspectives, or tools of inquiry become available.
Concept of justification: Beliefs are justified probabilistically on the basis of a variety of interpretive considerations, such as the weight of the evidence, the explanatory value of the interpretations, the risk of erroneous conclusions, consequences of alternative judgments, and the interrelationships of these factors. Conclusions are defended as representing the most complete, plausible, or compelling understanding of an issue on the basis of the available evidence.

"One can judge an argument by how well thought-out the positions are,
what kinds of reasoning and evidence are used to support it, and how consistent
the way one argues on this topic is as compared with other topics."

From King and Kitchener, 1994.

Few undergraduate students evidence truly reflective thinking at the most advanced stages, 6 and 7. However, reasoning at the highest stages is characteristic of advanced graduate students. "These stages reflect the epistemic assumption that one's understanding of the world is not 'given' but must be actively constructed and that knowledge must be understood in relationship to the context in which it was generated" (King and Kitchener, 1994, p. 17). At these stages evidence becomes an important criterion for judgments and the evidence must also be evaluated to determine its validity; some views may be evaluated as being more reasonable or more plausible. "Criteria that might be used in making such evaluations include conceptual soundness, coherence, degree of fit with the data, meaningfulness, usefulness and parsimony" (p. 17).

Although the reflective judgment model provides an important foundation for understanding moral development, it does not tell the whole story. In order for students to develop the ability to make more complicated and abstract judgments about ill-structured issues, educators must "create and sustain learning environments conducive to the thoughtful consideration of controversial topics, . . . help students learn to evaluate others' evidence-based

interpretations and . . . provide supportive opportunities for students to practice making and explaining their own judgments about important and complicated problems" (King, 1996, p. 232). Opportunities can be provided in
classrooms, in student activities, and in other types of experiential learning
environments. How does this foundational cognitive ability fit in an overall
view of college students' moral and ethical development? Rest (1984, 1994)
has proposed a four-component model of moral development that describes
moral behavior as consisting of moral sensitivity, moral motivation, moral character, and moral judgment. The following section gives an overview of this
model and places cognitive development in moral development framework.

Rest's Four-Component Model of Morality

Rest's Four-Component Model (1984, 1994) describes the determination of moral
behavior. Morality is considered a multifaceted phenomenon that goes beyond
the development of moral judgment. This model is considered "the single most
important theoretical advance in the field since Kohlberg's theory of moral development" (King, 1992, p. 4). The major determinants of moral behavior identified in this model were formulated from the morality literature in the fields of
cognitive-developmental, social learning, behavioristic, psychoanalytic, and social
psychological approaches. The model gives educators in higher education a more
comprehensive view of morality and a larger variety of interventions and contexts
from which moral development may be influenced than a single-dimensional
model (such as one focusing solely on moral judgment) might provide.

Rest (1984) asserts that "one-variable theories of morality are as untenable
as one-variable theories of personality . . . [since] two people who are similar
on one process need not be similar on other processes. A person who performs
one process with great facility need not have great facility on the other
processes" (p. 27). Each component is explained in detail below.

Component 1: Moral sensitivity. Moral sensitivity is the awareness of different
possible courses of action and how each could affect the welfare of all the parties
involved. It entails interpreting the situation and identifying a moral problem.

Research has shown that many people have great difficulty interpreting the
moral dimensions of even relatively simple situations (Bebeau, Rest, and Yamoor,
1985; Staub, 1978; Schwartz, 1977). People also have "striking individual differences . . . in their sensitivity to the needs and welfare of others" (Rest, 1984).
The ability to make inferences about others' needs and wants and how one's own
actions may affect others develops over one's life span—individuals differ in their
ability to make these types of inferences. Situations may also arouse strong emotions that affect an individual's ability to empathize with others involved. These
"aroused affects are part of what needs to be interpreted in a situation, and therefore part of Component 1 processing" (Rest, 1984, p. 30).

Component 2: Moral judgment. This component involves a method of figuring out what one ought to do by justifying choices about which line of action
is more morally just, or right. It consists of formulating a plan of action that

applies the relevant moral standard or ideal, what *ought* to be done in the situation. It is the component that Kohlberg's (1969) work on the stages of moral judgment advanced.

One approach to determining what the "moral ought" is in a particular situation is the social norm approach. A variety of social norms (such as social responsibility, equity, reciprocity, and the norm of giving) can be brought to bear on defining a moral course of action. In this approach, "moral development is a matter of acquiring a number of social norms and being set to have those norms activated by specific situations, as they arise" (Rest, 1984, p. 31). In contrast, the cognitive-development approach focuses on the purposes and workings of social arrangements (Rest, 1984). In this approach, development consists of the individual's increased awareness of various schemes of cooperation (or "stages" of moral reasoning), each characterized by its distinctive notion of the "possibilities and requirements for arranging cooperation among successively wider circles of participants" (p. 31). A specific moral dilemma is viewed from a generalized structure of obligations and rights.

Kohlberg's and Piaget's work has often been viewed as providing a total theory of moral development. However, Rest asserts that "reasoning about justice is no more the whole of morality than is empathy" (p. 32). In the Four-Component Model, moral judgment is viewed as an answer to the component 2 question, How do people define what is moral? A moral judgment theory does not "tell us how sensitive the person is even to noticing moral problems. It does not tell us what other values may preempt or compromise one's moral ideals, nor does it tell us how well a person is able to carry through on one's moral convictions" (p. 32).

Component 3: Moral motivation. Moral motivation is the importance given to moral values in comparison with competing values. Moral decisions often require choices among competing values. Are moral values given priority over other values (such as political sensitivity, professional aspiration, legality, public relations impact, financial security, self-actualization, protecting one's organization)? It is "not unusual for nonmoral values to be so strong and attractive that a person chooses a course of action that preempts or compromises the moral ideal" (Rest, 1984, p. 32). This component involves an evaluation of the various courses of action, their relationships to moral values, and their impact on action. Sometimes the choice of a moral alternative involves sacrificing some personal interest or enduring hardship.

Component 4: Moral character. This component involves "ego strength, perseverance, backbone, toughness, strength of conviction, and courage" (Rest and Narvaez, 1994, p. 24). It is the psychological toughness and strong character needed to execute and implement a line of action identified as morally desirable. This involves "figuring out the sequence of concrete actions, working around impediments and unexpected difficulties, overcoming fatigue and frustration, resisting distractions and other allurements, and not losing sight of the eventual goal" (Rest, 1984, p. 33). Inner strength, the ability to self-regulate and mobilize oneself to action, is vital for producing moral behavior.

The components are processes involved in the production of a moral act—not general traits or virtues. Each has a cognitive and an affective side. Though one process may interact with and influence another process, each performs a different function and is distinct from the other processes. All four components are determinants of moral action, and therefore moral failure can result from deficiency in any component:

> If a person is insensitive to the needs of others, or if a situation is too ambiguous to interpret, the person may fail to act morally (deficient in Component 1). Or a person may be deficient in formulating a moral course of action or may have simplistic and inadequate moral reasoning (Component 2). Or moral values can be compromised or preempted by other values (Component 3). Or it may be that a person has decided on a moral course of action but loses sight of the goal, is distracted, or just wears out (Component 4). (Rest, 1984, p. 36)

These four components, taken together, provide a much more comprehensive view of the psychology of morality than does moral judgment alone. Rest's model shows how the pieces fit together and provides a framework for understanding what it takes to succeed in performing a moral act (or, conversely, the different reasons why a person might fail to behave morally).

Interpretative Systems for Determining the Moral Ideal

The Four-Component Model describes moral judgments as the product of component 2, traditionally associated with Kohlberg's justice-based system. See Table 2.2. Thoma (1994) noted that other interpretative systems might inform or influence the way people arrive at a moral judgment. For example, Noddings has proposed an approach that places human caring as the foundation of ethical response. Noddings's view begins with the moral attitude of longing for goodness but "does not imply either that logic is to be discarded" (1984, p. 2). Rather than being based on universal principles and their application, the reasons given for moral actions in Noddings' framework "often point to feelings, needs, impressions, and a sense of personal ideal" (p. 3). Hers is a practical ethics of reciprocity based on ethical caring, a striving to meet the other person morally. Although both her ethics and the resulting recommendations she makes for moral education rest on a foundation of affective relation, Noddings acknowledges the role of thinking and reasoning in ethical conduct. She underscores that an individuals' "best thinking" should be used in determining a caring response. She refers to *ethical affect,* a process that acknowledges the interaction of cognition and feeling in the creation of an ethical response to the other. "Rationality, while important and prized, must serve something higher" (p. 172), the maintenance and enhancement of caring.

Table 2.2. Kohlberg's Theory of Moral Judgment

Level I: *Preconventional*—an egocentric perspective that derives moral constructs from individual needs.
Stage 1—*Obedience and punishment orientation*
Single concrete category for good and bad. Good gets rewarded; bad gets punished.
Stage 2—*Naively egoistic orientation*
Two concrete categories of morality. For me, good is what I want. For you, good is what you want. Bad is what is not wanted.

Level II: *Conventional*—based on the shared norms and values that sustain relationships, groups, communities, and societies.
Stage 3—*'Good boy' orientation*
Several concrete categories of morality are interrelated. Good is being considerate, nice, kind. Bad is being inconsiderate, mean, and unkind. This is true for self and others.
Stage 4—*Law-and-order orientation*
Morality is understood as a single abstraction. Laws are understood as a mechanism for coordinating expectations about acceptable and unacceptable behavior in communities.

Level III: *Postconventional*—reflective perspective on societal values in which moral principles that are universal in application are constructed.
Stage 5—*Contractual legalistic orientation*
Two or more abstract concepts of morality can be related. The moral framework from one context (such as a community's laws or standards of conduct) can be related to the moral framework in another context (those of another community).
Stage 6—*Conscience or principle orientation*
Abstract concepts of morality are understood as a system. Fairness of a given law may be interpreted differently, but the well-being of people is a common consideration. Principles such as the value of human life, justice, serving others, and contributing to the common good unify diverse concepts of morality.

Adapted from Kohlberg, 1969; Pascarella and Terenzini, 1991; King and Kitchener, 1994.

Gilligan (1977, 1982) also proposed a model of moral judgment based on care and responsibility for others rather than on justice and rights. The hierarchy of stages that make up this model is summarized in Table 2.3. In Gilligan's view the moral problem arises from conflicting responsibilities rather than conflicting rights. Its resolution depends on contextual and inductive thinking rather than formal and abstract reasoning. In this approach the primary moral concern is the infliction of hurt in particular moral situations. It contrasts with Kohlberg's morality of justice based on reciprocity and rights, in that it is based on a concept of harmony and nonviolence that recognizes the need for compassion and care for self and others. However, there is still a clear emphasis on using complex thought processes to reach the moral ideal.

Much has been written about the different moral orientations of the sexes. Brabeck examined the empirical evidence presented in research on sex differences in moral judgment and concluded that it "does not fully support . . . that males and females differed in moral orientation" (1983, p. 286). Brabeck offered another interpretative strategy that combines the contributions of Gilligan's theory and Kohlberg's model into a more integrated framework. At the heart of her approach is a distinction between the ideal and the real, the ethical principle

Table 2.3. Gilligan's Morality of Responsibility

Level I: *Orientation to individual survival.* Centers on self with a pragmatic concern for individual survival; morality is often viewed as sanctions imposed by a society in which individual is a subject, not a citizen.

First transition—*From selfishness to responsibility.* The transitional issue is attachment or connection to others; "selfishness" of willful decision making is counterposed to "responsibility" of moral choice.

Level II: *Goodness as self-sacrifice.* Moral judgment is equated to shared norms and expectations; goodness is the overriding concern because survival depends on acceptance by others.

Second transition—*From goodness to truth.* The transitional issue is a recognition that a morality of care must include care of self as well as care of others; morality begins to be assessed in terms of intentions and consequence, not from the eyes of others.

Level III: *Morality of nonviolence.* Care becomes the universal obligation and nonviolence is recognized as the principle governing all moral judgment and action; self and others are seen as moral equals to whom the injunction against hurting must be equally applied.

Adapted from Gilligan, 1977, 1982.

and the ethical act. Brabeck asserts that the moral 'ought' should be rationally defensible and should consider both principles and context. The moral imperative is determined absolutely, but the differences existing in any given situation or context influence our emotional response and choice of moral action. Thus, she suggests that Kohlberg's theory addresses a component 2 issue in Rest's model, judgment of the ideal; Gilligan speaks to components 1 and 3, the contextually relative responses to the specific individuals affected by one's moral choices. Brabeck's conception is of an expanded notion of morality that includes concern for interconnection, harmony, and nonviolence and redefines what constitutes an adequate description of the moral ideal. It defines the moral person "as one whose moral choices reflect reasoned and deliberate judgments that ensure [that] justice be accorded each person while maintaining a passionate concern for the well-being and care of each individual" (p. 289).

Each of these models exemplifies interpretative systems that can be used to inform moral judgments. Thus component 2 processes should be viewed as not only incorporating Kohlberg's judgment processes but also containing other interpretative systems as well (Thoma, 1994). Brabeck's approach also suggests that these interpretative systems can influence other components of the model. Another example is Noddings's discussion of what it means to act as "one-caring," which also has specific component 1 implications: sensitivity toward the welfare, protection, or enhancement of another may vary dramatically between individuals.

Returning to the Case of Tolerance

How do these theoretical constructs inform our understanding of a specific ethical issue? Let us return to the specific case of tolerance and apply these constructs. Guthrie (1996) explored the question of why some college students are more tolerant of diversity than others. She investigated the contribution of higher-order thinking skills to an individual's ability to make reasoned responses to others on the basis of evidence or contextual information in the context at hand, rather than on the basis of stereotypes. She found that an individual's ability to exhibit a nonprejudiced (or tolerant) response was related to his or her level of intellectual development as indicated by the capacity to make reflective judgments. Thus, reflective thinkers were more likely than individuals utilizing pre-reflective or quasi-reflective reasoning to reject a stereotype as an adequate or sufficient basis for their positions toward different others. More reflective thinkers also tended to be better able to divorce themselves from various influences (for example, parental, religious, stereotypical, societal) on their thinking in order to weigh and evaluate evidence, thus bringing their own reasoning abilities to bear and constructing their own solution. This conclusion implies that efforts in higher education to develop and build students' reflective thinking ability both in and out of the classroom are likely to have an accompanying positive impact on their tolerance levels.

Guthrie also concluded that level of intellectual development does not completely predict tolerance. This is consistent with Devine's model of prejudice and stereotyping (1989), on which Guthrie's study was based, and underscores the moral and ethical dimension of the issue. Rest's Four-Component Model provides a framework for understanding additional dimensions of tolerance. Component 1, moral sensitivity, requires that individuals be aware of the ethical dimensions of the situation that necessitate a tolerant response. They must identify the situation as moral and recognize that they have the potential to act in a manner that could affect the interests, welfare, or expectations of others. They must also be able to recognize the effect that their emotional response to the situation may have on their ability to empathize. College students may not be fully aware of situations in which prejudice and stereotyping affect their responses to others. Educators can develop interventions to sensitize students to these critical aspects of their relations with others.

Component 2, moral judgment, involves determining the moral ideal, or what one ought to do. As discussed above, the intellectual capacity to deal with complex, ill-structured issues is an important element in this process. There are various interpretative systems (several of which have been presented in this chapter) that inform or influence the way individuals arrive at a moral judgment and thus at the decision of how to evaluate or respond to difference. Pascarella and Terenzini (1991) have found "strong evidence to indicate that college positively influences the use of principled reasoning in judging moral issues" (p. 363). They have also cited an impressive amount of evidence that positively and systematically links more advanced, complex moral reasoning with moral behavior among college students. An individual's ability to tolerate diversity and to respect and appreciate human differences depends greatly on the ability to make a more complex and principled moral judgment within the framework of the individual's chosen interpretative strategy. Educators can intervene in ways that influence college student's moral judgment development and can expose college students to the various interpretative strategies for informing a moral judgment.

Component 3, moral motivation, requires giving priority to nonprejudiced, or tolerant, responses over competing values or different responses. Values such as peer acceptance or political sensitivity may affect what an individual decides to do in a situation involving a person who is significantly different. Elevating the moral ideal over nonmoral values such as personal comfort, peer acceptance, or expedience is no small undertaking, especially when such actions do not conform to institutional or peer group norms (King, 1992). Educators can aid students in recognizing the difficulty of behaving consistently with the moral ideal and make students more aware of the weighing process involving competing values that influence the decision of what to do. Explicit identification of the nonmoral value that is being elevated above the moral ideal may stimulate a reevaluation of the decision, a search for a new way to interpret the complex realities that reconciles the discordant perspectives, or an effort to identify alternative courses of action that encompass the competing values.

Component 4, moral character, involves the strength of conviction and courage to implement the moral ideal—in this case, to behave in a tolerant manner. It requires inner strength and a commitment to perform consistently in the course of action that will uphold the moral ideal. Students who have embraced values of equality and respect for human differences can use encouragement and support when these values are put to the test. To the extent that the culture of the campus community and the institutional and peer group norms support civility and appreciation of diversity, students' moral courage in situations calling for tolerance will be sustained. Educators can "affirm what is just and humane and use the instrumentalities of precept and example to bring others to the same affirmation" (Banner, 1980). Role modeling on the part of faculty and staff can be a powerful teaching tool in moral education. "Decisions to evade a moral issue or to arrive at an accommodation of convenience that is ethically marginal are no less powerful as teaching devices than thoughtful and morally courageous actions are" (Canon, 1985, p. 7). Educators can model ethical thinking and behavior and provide supportive environments for peer groups or student organizations that value and respect human differences.

Case Examples

The following case examples provide two specific instances of ethical dilemmas faced by today's college students. The discussion analyzes the situations on the basis of the above outlined theoretical constructs and shows how these models and principles can guide the development of specific interventions and purposeful educational activities to challenge and support college students' ethical development.

A student is working on a computer in a public worksite in the university library. She glances up from her research paper and sees, on a computer just two workstations away, another student working on a text document that he has surrounded with pictures of provocatively posed nude women in the screen space beside his document. She is uncomfortable, offended, and embarrassed.

What are the rights of the individual students involved in this situation? And what are their responsibilities to others in the learning environment? At the core of this dilemma is the issue of the limits to individual empowerment, because "individuals within a university community must be generally empowered to select—without university censorship—what they need to access for their learning, teaching, research, and personal purposes" (Rezmierski, 1995, p. 42). However, there is a competing interest for students to be able to work and learn in the campus environment free from being threatened, intimidated, embarrassed, or harassed. Therefore, the right of an individual to access material must be balanced against another individual's right to choose not to access or be exposed to material that is offensive or intimidating.

In this case, as in many, the offending student may simply be unaware of the effect of his actions on others—the insensitivity may be quite unconscious. Thus, this dilemma can be approached from a component 1, moral sensitivity, perspective. Perhaps simply raising awareness of the effects of the student's actions on others sharing the computer facilities can accomplish the intended objectives, especially if the offense was unintentional. However, it is possible that the intrusion into the private, personal, work, and psychological space of others was quite intentional. Although such actions are sometimes intended for comic or shock value, the action may have been specifically contrived to intimidate, threaten, or harass through a purposeful intrusion with material that the individual anticipates others will find offensive (Rezmierski, 1995). Pornography is only one type of material that can be considered offensive; racist, homophobic, or anti-Semitic materials would also fall into this category. Even if the act was intentional, moral sensitivity can still be a point of departure from which to approach this situation. Many students may not be fully aware of the psychological impact such an action may have on others or of how it might interfere with others' learning.

Rezmierski asserts that the topic of electronic access to potentially offensive material is one "around which learning and teaching can be built. It is an opportunity to teach and reinforce essential liberties while empowering all individuals" (1995, p. 44). The discussion of First Amendment rights, censorship, academic freedom, and essential individual liberties in universities and colleges must also include considerations of the community's values, the effects of an individual's intrusion on another, and the "disempowering of some individuals within the community as the expense for empowering others" (p. 44). Through educational discussion and debate of the competing interests and values involved in this issue, students can both increase their component 1 moral sensitivity to this ethical dilemma and glimpse vantage points held by others using different interpretative systems and levels of complexity in component 2 moral judgment.

In many instances such as this, responsibility will fall on a student affairs administrator to intervene and seek a successful resolution of the complex issues and competing interests involved. In cases in which potential harm has or is about to occur, administrators are obligated to stop the potentially harmful situation first and deal with the educational implications of the action for all parties involved subsequently. The administrator must bring his or her own ethical framework to bear on the decision, balancing the sometimes conflicting ethical and nonmoral principles that arise from considerations of the context of the institution, institutional rules and regulations, the legal rights of the students, and the many other situational factors that must also be considered in the decision.

> A student brings his date home from a party at which they have both consumed more than their usual limit of alcohol. They have been seeing each other exclusively for several months and have discussed becoming more physically intimate. At dinner prior to the party, she had hinted that "tonight might be the night" and he had also expressed a readiness to take the next step in the relationship. But he is now uncertain as to whether her responsiveness to his advances are truly consenting or largely alcohol induced. He does not want to endanger the relationship or jeopardize his own values by forcing sex on his girlfriend in a situation where she is not equally willing.

Unfortunately, relationship violence and sexual assault, which are exacerbated when combined with misuse of alcohol, are prevalent issues on our college campuses. In this situation it seems that component 1 and component 2 issues have already been considered. The student is sensitive to the dilemma he faces and the possible consequences his actions might have. He also seems to have used his own moral judgment to reach the conclusion that sex that is not mutually consented to is wrong or immoral. At stake in this situation are component 3 and 4 issues, moral motivation and moral character. Among competing values that might influence the student's decision of what to do are pressure from peer group norms and desire for physical satisfaction. And, provided the student chooses to act consistently with what he has determined to be the moral course of action, he must still have the strength of conviction to follow through with his plan of action.

According to Chickering and Reisser (1993), although interpersonal relationships "offer fertile ground for values exploration" (p. 243), students may have an easier time determining what their moral obligations are than applying them—especially in complex relationships. "Sexual attraction seems to be the great confounder of earlier vows" (p. 256). Add large doses of alcohol, and the situation becomes even more challenging. "Many students know perfectly well what they 'should' do, but faced with real-life pressures and temptations, they revert to what is most comfortable or self-protective" (p. 254).

Educators can help students identify the nonmoral values that often compete with their moral values and help them learn to weigh these contrasting values in a more explicit and considered manner, rather than automatically. Educators can also support and encourage students' development of moral character by modeling ethical behavior. According to Canon and Brown (1985), this involves not "self-righteous posturing" (p. 82) but rather a recognition that although each of us falls short of any ultimate ideal, we can still continually strive to achieve a higher level of ethical functioning. Educators can also contribute to an ethical climate that reinforces students' moral character by championing individual students' and student groups' moral causes (such as the International Peace Student Organization, the Men Against Rape group, and programming on multicultural awareness).

To lessen the likelihood of dealing with situations such as this one in disciplinary or counseling sessions after the fact, student affairs administrators must take action through avenues such as policy development, educational programming, and training. Addressing the issues of respectful relationships and ethical decision making through an integrated approach helps to create an ethical climate on campus that reinforces the student's moral motivation and moral character. Orientation programs or "University 101" freshman seminars provide opportunities to explore the ethical complexities of sexual behavior and decision making and the difficulties involved in "doing the right thing." Training for volunteers and student leaders can be structured to engage very influential peer group members such as resident assistants and peer sex educators in the creation of a campus climate that encourages ethical decisions and moral actions.

Conclusion

Brown (1985) asserts that the mission of the student affairs profession is to be the "moral conscience of the campus" (p. 68) by promoting and supporting ethical behavior on campus and recognizing and confronting unethical behavior. The advances in theory and applied research over the past twenty-five years on college students' moral development have resulted in a body of knowledge that is no longer speculative or theoretical. Student affairs educators have a professional responsibility to be aware of this knowledge and apply it in their practice.

This chapter underscores the reality that "the pursuit of ethical truths and the sustaining of ethical behaviors are intellectually demanding tasks. These efforts are also emotionally demanding; they require high levels of personal courage and a substantial measure of persistence" (Canon and Brown, 1985, p. 81). An understanding of college students' intellectual development, especially their capacity to deal with complex and ill-structured problems, will enhance our educationally purposive interventions aimed at developing students' ability to deal with challenging ethical dilemmas. In addition, viewing morality from the wider perspective of Rest's Four-Component Model, which goes beyond the singular process of moral judgment, holds great potential for increasing the diversity and effectiveness of our moral development efforts.

The Student Learning Imperative (American College Personnel Association, 1996) calls on student affairs professionals to intentionally create the conditions that enhance student learning and personal development. The literature offers many suggestions and provides examples of moral education interventions and educationally purposive activities in which students can be engaged throughout their college learning experience. The Four-Component Model can be used as a guide for planning moral education interventions of each the following types:

Direct experience with reflection. Service learning is an excellent example of this type of intervention, which centers on immediate experience and active problem solving and must be accompanied by an opportunity for reflection in which the individual creates a cognitive framework of understanding for the experience (see Romer, 1992).

Direct teaching. Some elements of the moral problem solving process can be taught directly, for example, basic logical and philosophical elements (see Penn, 1990). In addition, students can be taught about the processes involved in morality (such as the four components) and the influences on each process.

Developmental instruction. Both curricular and cocurricular interventions can be structured in ways that are aimed at developing the individual's capacity to make independent, reasoned judgments about complex issues (see King and Kitchener, 1994; Kroll, 1992a, 1992b; Kronholm, 1996; Strange, 1992). In addition, interventions can be designed that are specifically intended to develop an individual's capacities in other components (such as moral sensitivity; Bebeau, 1994).

Environmental or cultural interventions. The broader academic context can do much to augment the student experience toward moral development. A moral atmosphere or "ethical climate" (Brown, 1985) can be created that supports and reinforces the development of ethical reasoning and action in college students, for example, the just community approach; Kohlberg, 1985; Ignelzi, 1990).

Role modeling and ethical advocacy. Individual members of the campus community can serve as role models or ethical advocates. They can model ethical behavior and a continual striving for ethical ideals through their relationships with others and their decisions on practical matters and policy issues. In addition, as ethical advocates they can "raise relevant ethical questions, challenge reasoning, and advocate compelling ethical positions" (Ignelzi, 1990).

Subsequent chapters in this book provide further examples of intentionally designed moral education interventions that illustrate theory-based practice toward the ethical development of college students.

References

American College Personnel Association. "The Student Learning Imperative: Implications for Student Affairs." *Journal of College Student Development,* 1996, 37 (2), 118–122.

Banner, W. "The Moral Philosopher Looks at Values Education." In M. L. McBee (ed.), *Rethinking College Responsibilities for Values.* New Directions for Higher Education, no. 31. San Francisco: Jossey-Bass, 1980.

Baxter Magolda, M. B. *Knowing and Reasoning in College: Gender-related Patterns in Students' Intellectual Development.* San Francisco: Jossey-Bass. 1992

Bebeau, M. "Influencing the Moral Dimensions of Dental Practice." In J. Rest and D. Narvaez (eds.), *Moral Development in the Professions: Psychology and Applied Ethics.* Hillsdale, N.J.: Lawrence Erlbaum, 1994.

Bebeau, M., Rest, J., and Yamoor, C. "Measuring Dental Students' Ethical Sensitivity." *Journal of Dental Education,* 1985, 49 (4), 225–235.

Belenky, M., Clinchy, B., Goldberger, N., and Tarule, J. *Women's Ways of Knowing.* New York: Basic Books, 1986.

Bok, D. "Ethics, the University, and Society." *Harvard Magazine,* May–June 1988, 39–50.

Bok, D. *Universities and the Future of America.* Durham, N.C.: Duke University Press, 1990.

Bowling Green State University. *Undergraduate Catalog.* Bowling Green, Ohio: Bowling Green State University, 1993.

Brabeck, M. "Moral Judgment: Theory and Research on Differences Between Males and Females." *Developmental Review,* 1983, 3, 274–291.

Brown, R. D. "Creating an Ethical Community." In H. J. Canon and R. D. Brown (eds.), *Applied Ethics in Student Services.* New Directions for Student Services, no 30. San Francisco: Jossey-Bass, 1985.

Brown, R. D., and Canon, H. J. "Intentional Moral Development as an Objective of Higher Education." *Journal of College Student Personnel,* 1978, 426–429.

Brubacher, J., and Rudy, W. *Higher Education in Transition.* New York: Harper & Row, 1976.

Canon, H. J. "Ethical Problems in Daily Practice." In H. J. Canon and R. D. Brown (eds.), *Applied Ethics in Student Services.* New Directions for Student Services, no 30. San Francisco: Jossey-Bass, 1985.

Canon, H. J., and Brown, R. D. "How to Think About Professional Ethics." In H. J. Canon and R. D. Brown (eds.), *Applied Ethics in Student Services.* New Directions for Student Services, no. 30. San Francisco: Jossey-Bass, 1985.

Chickering, A. W., and Reisser, L. *Education and Identity.* (2nd ed.) San Francisco: Jossey-Bass. 1993.

Colby, A., and Kohlberg, L. *The Measurement of Moral Judgment.* Vol. 1: *Theoretical Foundations and Research Validation.* New York: Cambridge University Press, 1989.

Devine, P. "Stereotypes and Prejudice: Their Automatic and Controlled Components." *Journal of Personality and Social Psychology,* 1989, 56 (1), 5–18.

Garrison, J., Rud, A., Jr. "Introduction." In J. Garrison and A. Rud, Jr. (eds.), *The Educational Conversation: Closing the Gap.* Albany: State University of New York Press, 1995.

Gilligan, C. (1977). "In a Different Voice: Women's Conception of the Self and of Morality." *Harvard Educational Review,* 1977, 44, 481–517.

Gilligan, C. *In a Different Voice: Psychological Theory and Women's Development.* Cambridge, Mass.: Harvard University Press, 1982.

Guthrie, V. L. "The Relationship of Levels of Intellectual Development and Levels of Tolerance for Diversity Among College Students." Unpublished doctoral dissertation, Bowling Green State University, Ohio, 1996.

Ignelzi, M. "Ethical Education in a College Environment: The Just Community Approach." *NASPA Journal,* 1990, 27 (3), 192–198.

King, P. "Assessing Development from a Cognitive Developmental Perspective." In D. Creamer (ed.), *College Student Development: Theory and Practice for the 1990s.* Alexandria, Va.: ACPA Media, 1990.

King, P. "Creating Environments for Moral Development." *Proceedings of the 1992 Florida State University Institute on College Student Values.* Tallahassee: Florida State University, 1992.

King, P. "Student Cognition and Learning." In S. R. Komives, D. B. Woodard, Jr., and Associates. *Student Services: A Handbook for the Profession.* (3rd ed.) San Francisco: Jossey-Bass, 1996.

King, P., and Kitchener, K. *Developing Reflective Judgment: Understanding and Promoting Intellectual Growth and Critical Thinking in Adolescents and Adults.* San Francisco: Jossey-Bass, 1994.

King, P., Kitchener, K., and Wood, P. "The Development of Intellect and Character: A Longitudinal Study of Intellectual and Moral Development in Young Adults." *Moral Education Forum,* 1985, *10* (1), 1–13.

King, P., Kitchener, K., Wood, P., and Davison, M. "Relationships Across Developmental Domains: A Longitudinal Study of Intellect, Moral, and Ego Development." In M. Commons, J. Sinnott, F. Richards, and C. Armon (eds.), *Adult Development.* New York: Praeger, 1989.

Kitchener, K. "Human Development and the College Campus: Sequences and Tasks." In G. Hanson (ed.), *Measuring Student Development.* New Directions for Student Services, no. 20. San Francisco: Jossey-Bass, 1982.

Kitchener, K., and King, P. "Reflective Judgment: Concepts of Justification and Their Relationship to Age and Education." *Journal of Applied Developmental Psychology,* 1981, 2 (2), 89–116.

Kohlberg, L. "Stage and Sequence: The Cognitive Developmental Approach to Socialization." In D. Goslin (ed.), *The Handbook of Socialization Theory and Research.* Chicago: Rand McNally, 1969.

Kohlberg, L. *Essays on Moral Development.* Vol. 1: *The Philosophy of Moral Development.* San Francisco: Harper & Row, 1981.

Kohlberg, L. *The Psychology of Moral Development: The Nature and Validation of Moral Stages.* San Francisco: Harper and Row, 1984.

Kohlberg, L. "The Just Community Approach to Moral Education in Theory and Practice." In M. Berkowitz and F. Oser (eds.), *Moral Education: Theory and Application.* Hillsdale, N.J.: Lawrence Erlbaum, 1985.

Kroll, B. "Reflective Inquiry in a College English Class." *Liberal Education,* 1992a, *78* (1), 10–13.

Kroll, B. *Teaching Hearts and Minds: College Students Reflect on the Vietnam War in Literature.* Carbondale: Southern Illinois University Press, 1992b.

Kronholm, M. "The Impact of Developmental Instruction on Reflective Judgment." *Review of Higher Education,* 1996, *19* (2), 199–225.

Noddings, N. *Caring: A Feminine Approach to Ethics and Moral Education.* Berkeley: University of California Press, 1984.

Oberlin College. *Course Catalog.* Oberlin, Ohio: Oberlin College, 1992.

Pascarella, E. T., and Terenzini, P. T. *How College Affects Students: Findings and Insights from Twenty Years of Research.* San Francisco: Jossey-Bass, 1991.

Penn, W., Jr. "Teaching Ethics: A Direct Approach." *Journal of Moral Education,* 1990, *19* (2), 124–138.

Perry, W. *Forms of Intellectual and Ethical Development in the College Years: A Scheme.* New York: Holt, Rinehart and Winston, 1970.

Piaget, J. *The Moral Development of the Child.* London: Kegan Paul, 1932.

Rest, J. "The Major Components of Morality." In W. Kurtines and J. Gewirtz (eds.), *Morality, Moral Behavior, and Moral Development.* New York: Wiley, 1984.

Rest, J. "Why Does College Promote Development in Moral Judgment?" *Journal of Moral Education,* 1988, *17* (3), 183–194.

Rest, J. "Background: Theory and Research." In J. Rest and D. Narvaez (eds.), *Moral Development in the Professions: Psychology and Applied Ethics.* Hillsdale, N.J.: Lawrence Erlbaum, 1994.

Rest, J., Bebeau, M., and Volker, J. "An Overview of the Psychology of Morality." In J. Rest (ed.), *Moral Development: Advances in Research and Theory.* New York: Praeger, 1986.

Rest, J., and Narvaez, D. (eds.). *Moral Development in the Professions: Psychology and Applied Ethics.* Hillsdale, N.J.: Lawrence Erlbaum, 1994.

Rezmierski, V. "Computers, Pornography and Conflicting Rights." *Educom Review,* 1995, *30* (2), 42–44.

Romer, N. "A Feminist View of Moral Development: Criticisms and Applications." *Initiatives,* 1992, *54* (3), 19–32.

Sandeen, A. "The Legacy of Values Education in College Student Personnel Work." In J. Dalton (ed.), *Promoting Values Development in College Students.* NASPA Monograph Series, no. 4. Washington, D.C.: National Association of Student Personnel Administrators, 1985.

Schwartz, S. "Normative Influences on Altruism." In L. Berkowitz (ed.), *Advances in Experimental Social Psychology.* Vol. 10. New York: Academic Press, 1977.

Staub, E. *Positive Social Behavior and Morality.* New York: Academic Press, 1978.

Strange, C. "Beyond the Classroom: Encouraging Reflective Thinking." *Liberal Education,* 1992, *78* (1), 28–32.

Thoma, S. "Moral Judgments and Moral Action." In J. Rest and D. Narvaez (eds.), *Moral Development in the Professions: Psychology and Applied Ethics.* Hillsdale, N.J.: Lawrence Erlbaum, 1994.

Welfel, E. "Ethical Practice in College Student Affairs." In D. Creamer (ed.), *College Student Development: Theory and Practice for the 1990s.* Alexandria, Va.: American College Personnel Association, 1990.

VICTORIA L. GUTHRIE *is assistant professor of student personnel leadership at Ohio University.*

Thinking of ethical beliefs as firm guidelines is impossible in dynamic and complex situations. New processes must be developed to address ethical issues as part of all management decisions.

Ethics in Management

F. J. Talley

The landscape of higher education has changed dramatically in the past decade. Many four-year colleges and universities are faced with stable or declining enrollments, increased costs of personnel or other services, budget cuts, and significant new costs to build the technology infrastructure necessary to maintain or improve the quality of education for their students. Many institutions have not recovered from the demographic shifts of the late 1980s. Competition comes not only for limited pools of prospective students but also from prisons and highway projects because of limited state appropriations and politically attractive tax rebates.

Financial aid allocations from government sources have been significantly reduced in the last decade, and institutional financial aid resources, in what is known as tuition "discounting," have placed significant financial pressures on institutions of higher learning (Speck, 1996). Even in financially stable institutions, increasing competition for students requires ever more sophisticated and expensive recruiting techniques. For example, the "bells and whistles," such as expanded athletics facilities and technology centers, that used to be considered luxuries, are now seen as basic necessities. Few of these features are inexpensive. The conditions facing higher education today demand reflective practitioners (Schön, 1990) who can use their knowledge of a situation and its context to construct new and creative solutions to problems, rather than relying on rigid, outdated rules.

Young science students are often told that an animal with the size of a duck, the muscle structure of a duck, and the wingspread of a duck should not be able to fly—and yet ducks can fly. This example is intended to stimulate creative thinking—to teach students that unquestioning acceptance of scientific principles can limit insight and understanding. Administrators in colleges and universities who accept and try to use principles of management and leadership that were effective in earlier eras, and ignore the changing context of our times, face a difficult and uncertain future. In fact, some believe that the structure and systems of American higher education are woefully inadequate for the challenges of the twenty-first century (Cause, 1991).

The purpose of this chapter is to present an overview of some of the most recent approaches to management and to examine some of the ethical implications of using these approaches. Elements of these innovative systems will be applied in three cases that are both managerially and ethically complex. The new approaches require a great deal of dialogue among decision makers and assume that continuous change is normal. They also assume that awareness of the ethical dimension of decision making is part of the decision-making process. Using process-oriented, outcomes-based management is extremely challenging, particularly for people accustomed to systems governed by standard operating procedures that fail to address the long-term consequences of "business as usual" operating assumptions.

How would student affairs practitioners react when faced with possibilities such as eliminating the Division of Student Affairs and replacing division employees with faculty mentors, placing student affairs departments under the supervision of academic affairs, rewriting position descriptions to focus on customer service and treating students as customers, shifting positions from admissions to the athletic department to improve recruiting, or making a practitioner's salary dependent on the number of students he or she recruits to the institution? Although these changes may not be currently taking place at many institutions, they represent a challenge to the traditional ways of working on college and university campuses. These include challenges to traditional academic structures, budgeting and planning processes, long-held institutional priorities, and traditional notions of academic quality, including the definition, development, and measurement of quality. Each of these challenges carries ethical implications. Student affairs cannot avoid these challenges, but it can manage the process of addressing them and can actively debate the ethical issues they raise.

Several management and leadership systems have been developed to position organizations for future change. These systems, known variously as Total Quality Management (TQM), Total Quality Improvement (Cornesky, McCool, Byrnes, and Weber, 1991), Continuous Quality Improvement, Reengineering, and Force Field Analysis (Cornesky and McCool, 1992), have several elements in common, including a focus on customer service and satisfaction, continuous improvement, operational definition of quality, and continuous measurement of improvements in products and services. They all emphasize the involvement of workers in the analysis of work quality and the improvement of service. They are designed to transform institutions in basic and radical ways rather than to address short-term concerns.

All these management systems or approaches contain elements that can help colleges or universities solve problems, streamline services, and improve the quality of education for their students. But many in higher education are wary of management systems and methods, particularly those imported from business and industry. Few colleges and universities, for example, can be said to follow the prescriptions of TQM precisely, despite the fact that quality management principles such as collaboration and collegial governance are generally respected in higher education. For example, TQM assumes that everyone in an organization is able to contribute in the problem identification process and in the development of improvement strategies. These approaches also focus on students as the primary beneficiaries or "customers" of education, and make student service and student learning the prime institutional emphases. Finally, it is assumed that everyone involved in the process will continue to learn and improve their performance (Cornesky and McCool, 1992). All of these features are compatible with viewing colleges and universities as ethical communities that solve problems and deliver services in a manner consistent with their professional values.

Unfortunately, attempts to implement these systems and approaches to decision making and leadership often fail, for four primary reasons. One reason is that the institution fails to get agreement among community members on the mission, vision, and goals of the institution before implementing the new approach. Thus, different people and work groups start the process with different assumptions about what the institution stands for.

Another reason is that although these approaches to management and decision making are designed to improve the quality of education for students and improve services, they are usually undertaken as a way of cutting costs (Entin, 1994). Employees involved in the implementation of these processes are reluctant to commit themselves to an exercise they see as dishonest.

A third reason is that leaders are unable or unwilling to relinquish the level of control necessary for true implementation of the systems, calling into question their commitment to it.

Finally, leaders fail to recognize the training investment necessary for implementation of these systems (Entin, 1994).

Quality Management Approaches

What follows is a brief explanation of popular management and decision-making systems. Subsequent sections will present a detailed discussion of how management systems might be applied to the difficult issues facing our institutions, including discussion of the ethical implications of implementation.

Total Quality Management. TQM is defined as a "management-driven philosophy that encourages everyone in the organization to know the organization mission and to adopt a quality philosophy to continuously improve on how the work is done to meet the satisfaction of the customer" (Cornesky and McCool, 1992, p. 2). Although TQM is the most widely known of the quality management systems, it is not the only one. All these systems share similar strengths and weaknesses. Penrod and Dolence (1992) identified five major elements of TQM. First, the organization must focus on its customers, or those people or agencies the organization serves. Customer focus asserts that "the leadership of an organization must, by word and deed, convey the message that customer satisfaction, through a process of continually improving quality, is the responsibility of every member of the organization" (Grace and Templin, 1994, p. 75). In the case of higher education, that first constituency is alleged to be the students, although in practice it is often unclear or ambiguous. Second, TQM is designed to improve operations systematically, through the implementation of specific techniques. Third, to develop and implement quality improvement in the organization, human resources must be developed. Three specific areas for human resource development are mentioned: training to support changes in worker behavior, training for workers in creating positive changes in jobs and job structure, and assistance in modifying the culture of the organization so that change is encouraged (Penrod and Dolence, 1992). The fourth major element of TQM is the necessity for long-term thinking, and the fifth element is commitment to quality (Penrod and Dolence, 1992).

When institutions implement TQM, they solicit ideas and suggestions from members of the organization or people or agencies touched by the organization. For a business, customers and suppliers are solicited for suggestions on how to improve operations. In colleges and universities, many groups and individuals, including students, faculty members, staff members, employers, high school counselors, and parents, are questioned systematically to learn how to eliminate redundancies, improve the quality of services, speed up operations, and reorient services for the expressed needs of the various customers, or constituents (Cornesky and McCool, 1992). Colleges and universities form teams to solicit and evaluate suggestions for quality improvement or streamlining. The leaders themselves may serve on these teams, but they usually do not assume leadership roles. Cornesky and McCool caution that members of a work group often defer to the person in power, regardless of that person's designated role on the team. This problem is caused by contradictions between role expectations in shared responsibility systems such as TQM systems and more singular responsibility systems such as typical bureaucracies. Such a deferral can undermine the effectiveness of the process and stifle creativity. TQM also includes the use of a number of diagnostic tools, such as Cause and Effect Diagrams, Flow Charts, and Force Field Analysis to aid in problem identification and analysis and to help in developing strategies for improvement (Cornesky and McCool, 1992). These diagnostic tools are designed to determine the root causes of problems, identify possible solutions and solution systems, and illuminate the forces that support the solution of problems.

Proponents of quality management approaches believe that implementing these techniques will streamline processes, cut management levels, and reduce costs of providing services to customers. Businesses have often turned to quality management approaches to reduce costs and enhance competitive position rather than to provide better service as an end in itself. Therefore these approaches are often brought into businesses and higher education as a means of reducing the size of an organization and its staff and thereby reducing its costs (Entin, 1994). When any quality management system is used for purposes other than those that are publicly discussed, trust in the process is undermined. Lack of trust inevitably leads to lack of effectiveness in these situations.

Reengineering. Reengineering takes a more radical approach than quality management. Reengineering seeks to improve policies or procedures by challenging the culture and values of an organization in fundamental ways, not by making small changes in an organization's processes. Reengineering works for organizational transformation. The process of reengineering begins by defining and redefining an organization's culture: why it exists, and what its values and rewards, its purposes, and its assumptions about its present and future are (Cause, 1991). The reengineered workplace is designed to look and function very differently from its predecessor. Organizations that have reengineered would, in theory, have more decentralized functions, fewer levels of management, and fewer staff members. Professional management would be less important, and entrepreneurialism would be more highly valued. Employees would perform the multiple functions of teacher, learner, evaluator, designer, and steward (Cause, 1994). This is perhaps the most difficult part of reengineering. With TQM, people are encouraged to ask, How can we do this differently to serve our customers better? Reengineering encourages people to ask, How can I become different in order to serve our customers better?

The techniques used to reengineer are similar to the ones used in TQM: a variety of diagnostic tools such as flow charts and grids that aid in defining problems and developing solutions. Reengineering spends time examining the culture and the driving values of the organization as well as its processes. If a college or university were to undergo reengineering, basic questions would be asked: Why is 120 credit hours the proper amount for all of our degree programs? Why is it so important for students to take their last thirty credit hours in residence? What do we value so much about face-to-face contact with faculty that we do not teach any courses on the computer? What is so important about a residential experience that we maintain our residence halls? Why do we have tenure? What is academic freedom, and why do we value it? Whereas some of these questions may be asked using other management systems or processes, reengineering, with its propensity for challenging everything, has to ask them all.

While reengineering, one college decided to reduce its costs or increase revenues by 20 percent because that figure represented the amount of money that could not be saved by doing "business as usual." Fundamental changes included rewriting job descriptions, changing organizational procedures, and changing leadership style. Incremental change would not have produced the desired results. The college reengineering effort was not very successful. Participants generally agreed that the exercise was only successful in cutting some costs and in identifying a few revenue sources for growth. What the college did not do, however, was challenge the basic structure and culture of the institution, such as assumptions about how students are taught, or about the workload of its faculty. The process at the college was one of cost containment, with little attention paid in the final report on how to do things differently or on how employees might make themselves different to serve their customers better.

Inherent in the college's reengineering project was the assumption that if people simply worked harder at what they were already doing, they would be able to meet the challenges facing the institution. Peter Senge, in *The Fifth Discipline* (1990), suggests otherwise. Senge lists a number of rules that help managers recognize their interrelationships with other managers and with parts of their organizations—their relationship to institutional systems—so that they can think differently about their organization and about the solutions to its problems. This might be considered "reengineering plus"—a challenge to the basic assumptions about the organization and recognition that redefining the organization and positioning it for the future will require an understanding of and fundamental change in the systems that guide it.

According to Senge, the usual approaches that assume that simple short-term solutions will resolve most long-term systemic problems are flawed. "The harder you push"—the harder you work using the same assumptions, procedures, and systems—"the harder the system pushes back" (1990, p. 58). Senge's work encourages managers to challenge the foundations of their systems, since people placed in the same system tend to produce similar results. The system itself influences behavior and approaches to problem solving so much that the only way to position an organization for more radical change is to challenge the systems on which it is based. Senge explains systems of people and processes, believing that quality human relationships are an essential element of organizational success. Only systems thinking—understanding the complexity and interrelatedness of organizations, individuals, and processes and using an understanding of those systems to change them—can produce significant, long-term results. But these results do not come easily. Senge suggests that choosing easy solutions—an approach he calls shifting the burden or addressing the symptoms rather than the underlying causes of a problem—generally leads to more problems, some of which may be more difficult to resolve than the original one. Managers and others who have become accustomed to short-term results are often disappointed, since systems thinking is designed for long-term rather than short-term gains. But he argues that an organization that employs these new ways of thinking—the *learning organization*—is far more likely to survive in times of rapid change and economic unpredictability.

Framework for Ethical Practice

The American College Personnel Association has used a system of principle ethics as its framework for appropriate professional practice. The five principles, explained by Kitchener (1985), are respecting autonomy, doing no harm, benefiting others, being just, and being faithful. These principles help student affairs practitioners understand the minimum ethical standards by which professional behavior is judged. Meara, Schmidt, and Day (1996) have discussed the integration of virtue ethics with principle ethics to facilitate the development of ethical character and the habits of ethical behavior (Rion, 1989) that tend to support ethical practice. "Virtue ethics call upon individuals to aspire toward ideals and to develop virtues or traits of character that enable them to achieve these ideals" (p. 24). Principle ethics focuses on obligations and on behavior, whereas virtue ethics focuses on the ideals to which an individual might aspire, and on individual character. Principles might govern compliance with a racial quota, whereas virtue ethics would emphasize striving toward the higher goal of a multicultural organization. Adherence to a system of virtue ethics would encourage practitioners to focus on how they can change to become better professionals and worry less about individual incidents. In their understanding, "Principles inform one about what is morally good" (p. 29). Therefore, virtue ethics becomes most powerful when linked to ethical principles. In sum, principle ethics defines the science of ethical thinking, and virtue ethics shapes the art of ethical practice.

There are five significant characteristics of virtuous agents or practitioners (Meara, Schmidt, and Day, 1996): being motivated to do good; possessing vision and discernment; understanding the role of affect and emotion; self-awareness; and comprehending the community's ideal expectations, mores, and sensibilities. Each of these characteristics can be translated into behavior and used as a means of evaluating practitioners' performance in quality management, reengineering, or learning organizations. Failure to act in accordance with virtue ethics may undermine the effectiveness of these practices.

Motivation to do good is self-defining: a person is motivated to do good if doing good is his or her intention. Vision and discernment are more abstract. Discernment has been defined as "the ability to perceive the ethically relevant features of a given situation" (Meara, Schmidt, and Day, 1996, p. 29). Vision and discernment include "a tolerance for ambiguity, perspective taking, and an understanding of the links between current behavior and future consequences" (p. 29). Virtuous agents with discernment and vision are able to understand ethical principles, how to apply them, and how they are relevant to any given situation.

The third characteristic of virtuous agents is an understanding of the role of emotion in decision making and professional conduct. Virtuous agents are able to look at problems objectively while also acknowledging the importance of emotional reactions and feelings in carrying out professional practice. A common example of this virtue in action is permitting victims of campus sexual assaults to submit victim impact statements in campus disciplinary proceedings. Such statements are used to present the emotional reaction of the victim, which can be taken into account during the proceedings.

The fourth characteristic of virtuous agents is self-awareness. Through self-awareness, practitioners are able to avoid decision making or courses of action based on personal biases, prejudices, or assumptions. This understanding is a "prerequisite for effective cross cultural understanding" (Meara, Schmidt, and Day, 1996, p. 31). A process such as reengineering also requires self-awareness because it involves changing organizational culture and is comparable to developing cross-cultural understanding.

The final characteristic of virtuous agents is interdependence with the community "and comprehending the communities' ideal expectations, mores and sensibilities" (Meara, Schmidt, and Day, 1996, p. 31). Practitioners behaving ethically in this framework acknowledge their membership in the community and respect for its values, even while seeking to change them. Virtues, in contrast to principles, are meaningful only in a community context. (The role of community in virtue ethics is discussed more extensively by Fried in Chapter One of this volume.) For example, when implementing quality management approaches, practitioners are in effect espousing the values of the particular approach and attempting to create a community of shared values in the workplace. One such value in TQM is the importance of recognizing the contributions of every member of the community in the process. If college leaders fail to involve a segment of the campus community, such as part-time faculty, in quality work teams, the leaders are not acting in accordance with the values they have espoused and are therefore not acting as virtuous agents.

Some college or business leaders fail to follow the values and procedures inherent in the change process they design. When leaders implementing TQM hold separate meetings to evaluate the preliminary suggestions of quality work teams, they are acting outside the process, and therefore unethically. The same can be said of people who act outside the culture of the organization. Long-term, systemic change comes through changes in organizational culture, rather than through changes in isolated procedures, individual job descriptions, or the reporting lines of one or two departments (Childress and Senn, 1995), even though these changes may occur during the process of changing the culture in the broader sense. Colleges and universities that hire presidents to "shake things up" may find that the short-term changes are remarkable but that the institution reverts to its old way of doing things when that president leaves or when the pressure to do things a new way is removed. The affect of bureaucratic inertia and habit cannot be overstated. For example, a university cannot become "student centered" or embrace customer service in its financial or operations management areas like the bursar's office, the financial aide office, or the housing maintenance office overnight if the organizational culture has historically treated students with problems as inconveniences to the bureaucratic routine. Changes in attitudes and values must accompany changes in procedure and must be reshaped over the long term by rewards built into the employee evaluation systems. Only leaders who understand their institutional cultures can imagine and create methods for changing them. When performance expectations and rewards reflect institutional culture and values, employees are more likely to develop the virtues expected of them and to behave accordingly on the job. Ethical behavior becomes the most desirable behavior in the context.

Recognizing the integration of cognition and affect in bureaucratic systems is a particular problem in higher education. Senge (1990) emphasizes the importance of acknowledging the wholeness of human experience as one pillar of ethical practice in organizations. The values that shape scientific research are also powerful influences on the values that shape most university communities. Scientific values posit a split between thinking and feeling and elevate reason over emotion as the primary basis of decision making. These rational values shape both science and business (Fried, 1995). Reliance on quantitative data, whether generated as a research report or a financial report, often determines decisions about tenure, services for students, and a wide range of policies in the absence of any modifying qualitative considerations. In the old aphorism, "If the only tool you have is a hammer, everything looks like a nail." Quantitative methods are not designed to measure the integration of affect and cognition, but these are the tools that university faculty and administration members consider capable of generating the most credible results. The consequence is that universities have a great deal of difficulty measuring, or even defining, progress that takes affect, in the form of qualitative data, into account. How would one measure the effect of terminating ten part-time employees who are hired each semester to help students register for classes and replacing these employees with a telephone registration system that is accessed through push-button phones from any location? The speed and cost of registration could easily be compared under both systems. Measuring changes in student satisfaction and feelings of connection with the university would be considerably more difficult. If a university advertises itself as "student centered," which values should shape decisions about registration—impersonal, low-cost methods, or personal, more expensive methods? Should both methods be available? Is the university under any obligation to continue hiring these long-term, part-time employees? Should decisions about money be made purely on the principle of cost saving, or should some inclusionary process be used to make a decision that balances virtue and principle?

Theory to Practice

In situations with ethical implications, principle ethics helps identify the evaluation criteria for defining and addressing problems. Conformity to principles can be used to measure results. Virtue ethics, on the other hand, suggests that one aspires to the finest professional practice and requires that practitioners develop an internalized framework for reaching those aspirations. The discussion of the following two cases will focus on the ways in which a practitioner follows the virtue ethics framework of Meara, Schmidt, and Day (1996).

Two important issues facing colleges and universities today are affirmative action and free speech. Colleges and universities frequently fail when trying to address these issues because of their tendency to employ inappropriate systems or processes. These issues challenge our view of what colleges and universities are supposed to do and call into question the integrity of the institution as indicated by compliance with its espoused values. For example, speech codes, no matter how carefully crafted, are bound to offend those who believe any restriction of free expression to be counter to academic freedom. They ask, "Are colleges and universities to be places of free expression and exploration, or will a single standard of expression become predominant?"

The issues of affirmative action and free speech also bring considerations of just, ethical treatment and behavior into focus. Each, however, can and should be addressed in the college community. When doing so, practitioners are cautioned to avoid the pitfalls to implementation of management systems. These are as follows:

The institution fails to get agreement among community members on the mission, vision, and goals of the institution before implementation.
Management approaches are implemented to cut costs rather than to transform the institution (Entin, 1994).
Leaders are unable or unwilling to relinquish the level of control necessary for true implementation of the systems.
Leaders fail to recognize the training investment necessary for success (Entin, 1994, p. 7).

A Case of TQM and Affirmative Action. Affirmative action has divided faculties and governments and has been the focus of increasing scrutiny in our colleges and universities. In 1995 the University of California System Regents voted to end all racial and ethnic preferences in admissions and hiring. Since that vote, many in the higher education community in California and elsewhere have protested this change in policy and reaffirmed their commitment to affirmative action. The Supreme Court recently struck down the use of any affirmative action category as part of admission decisions at the University of Texas Law School. How can this issue be addressed on a college campus? Because the legal parameters that regulate affirmative action policies in higher education are becoming more narrowly defined and exclusionary, each campus must develop a community value system that acknowledges the integration of affect and cognition, encourages self-awareness, and creates consensus regarding the means by which diversity is to be treated (or ignored) on each campus.

Breakstone State College decided to develop a new affirmative action policy and has formed a committee of students, staff, and faculty members to write a new draft policy and procedure guidelines for admissions and hiring. President Gould, hoping to showcase this committee as an example of TQM procedures at work, gave the committee maximum latitude to craft the policy and procedures as it saw fit. She chose the committee members carefully on the basis of their clear thinking, ability to work in groups, and charisma. The president was known as a strong advocate of building a more diverse community, and she knew the committee members were committed to that as well.

The committee began its work on admissions policies and procedures and ran into trouble almost immediately. The students on the committee, including the president of the Black Student Union, wanted assurances that the college would respond to its mandate to educate the citizens of the state. The students spent more time talking about the need to eliminate racism among the faculty than about admissions or hiring procedures. "Is it fair," they wondered, "to admit students only to have them mistreated by the faculty?"

Most of the faculty on the committee wanted assurance that as few students as possible were admitted who did not meet the minimum standardized test and high school rank guidelines. They wanted a limit on the number of such students and to reserve those spots for students of color. "Is it just," they asked, "to admit students into the college who have no hope of graduating?"

Administrators on the committee were concerned about the fact that affirmative action beneficiaries tended to have higher levels of financial need than most other students. They wanted to include in their procedures new scholarship programs aimed at attracting and retaining under-privileged students with high academic potential. "What does it say about our college," they asked, "that we lure students into it only to force unreasonable loan burdens on them to cover the cost of their education?"

Another contingent, composed of two faculty members and an administrator, believed the other people had missed the mark. Since most recipients of affirmative action "benefits" were women, not necessarily people of color, they believed the policy and procedures should in some way address the feminization of the campus and how Breakstone State should respond to it. The admissions director, who served on the committee as an ex-officio member, threw up his hands and said, "Look, if you really want more minority students on this campus, I can get them—but I'm going to need a lot more money to travel to the urban areas these students come from."

The committee was unable to come to agreement on a single, focused affirmative action policy statement. It decided simply to reaffirm the college's stance against discrimination based on race, gender, ethnicity, sexual preference, disability, or age, and it included in its recommendations a list of new initiatives, with a hefty price tag. These recommendations included two new admissions positions for minority recruitment (total cost $100,000), increased admissions travel budget and materials (total cost $30,000), new scholarship aid (total cost $100,000), and diversity training for faculty and staff (total cost $25,000). The total cost of the recommendations would be $255,000.

When the final report was presented to President Gould at a committee meeting, she was silent for a while. Then she told the committee she was not pleased with their work, because they had not done what she had asked them to do—write a draft policy and procedure guidelines on affirmative action. Based on the document she had received, she still had no idea who Breakstone's students should be, what its community should look like, and how to justify the institution's stance on affirmative action, internally or externally. She asked them to try again and to return with a detailed explanation of what the initiatives were designed to accomplish and how they would fit into the college's mission and goals. The committee members, crestfallen that their ideas had been dismissed, went away angrily, wondering what they had done wrong.

In this scenario, the president was upset with the committee because it failed to do what she wanted them to do. Yet the president was inadvertently responsible for many of the committee's problems. The committee never understood the basic values or the mission and goals regarding affirmative action that the president believed they understood. For example, is affirmative action all about admitting more people of color who are different? Is it about providing opportunity to people who are less privileged? Is it about admitting more highly qualified students of different racial and ethnic backgrounds? These may not be mutually exclusive ideas, but they are clearly based on different values. If committee members entered the change process with such different perspectives regarding affirmative action at Breakstone State, they were bound to have problems coming to agreement.

In addition, the committee received very little preparation for its task and very little support or instruction during its activities. The president assumed that because the committee members shared a commitment to the idea of affirmative action, they would be able to work together and develop a new policy and procedure guidelines, and she ignored their need for support. They did not discuss the different understandings about affirmative action held by committee members or differences between the committee and the president. As the committee conducted its deliberations, the members should have realized how little agreement they had among themselves about basic issues and terms. A request for a midcourse meeting with the president would have assisted in clarification of their task and produced a more receptive environment for the final report.

The president also confounded the process she instituted. By tabling the recommendations of the committee, she implied that she was not truly committed to an open process of decision making. This will make it much harder for her to form other working committees in the future, because participants will know ahead of time that they will have little say in whether their recommendations are implemented.

A more effective alternative would have been for the president to help the committee define the relationship between the affirmative action policy and the institution's values, mission, and goals. This would have allowed the committee to place affirmative action in the context of institutional mission and goals. It would also have encouraged individual members to acknowledge their different perspectives on affirmative action. This approach would have permitted the committee to start its work with a common understanding of affirmative action, of the general direction in which it had to move, and of the obstacles it would face. Once this groundwork was laid, the process of discussing specific procedure guidelines would have been easier. This groundwork should also have included a detailed discussion of the relationship between affirmative action and quality. A little more conversation between the president and committee members prior to the beginning of the committee's work would have enhanced the likelihood of more satisfactory results and wider campus support for the final recommendations.

The change process being undertaken at Breakstone raised several ethical questions. Using the terminology of virtue ethics and virtuous agents, it can be assumed that the people on the committee were motivated to do what is good. But did they possess vision and discernment as individuals or as a body? If they were unable to perceive the ethically relevant features of the task, they would be likely to fail. A few such features were mentioned by the committee, such as the ethics of admitting students who were likely to fail without academic support systems and management of debt burden. Another ethically relevant feature was concern about the ill treatment of students in the classroom. After discussion of these issues, however, the committee did not advance to the next stage of discernment, that of linking current behavior to future consequences, and the interrelatedness of the issues (Meara, Schmidt, and Day, 1996). For example, are some faculty treating students poorly in the classroom out of frustration because the students are ill prepared for college work? It is the understanding of the interrelatedness of issues that characterizes true discernment. The committee should also have considered the role of emotion in the college community. Developing a new system to make students of color feel welcome on the campus while at the same time ignoring their anger is unlikely to succeed. Similarly, failing to acknowledge the valid frustration of faculty in teaching poorly prepared students is unlikely to garner faculty support for the proposed solution.

Virtuous agents are also self-aware. Many members on the committee discussed their concerns and perspectives freely, but there was little effort to confront biases and prejudices. One reason the committee had difficulty writing a new draft policy was that members had failed to understand and work through their individual prejudices and biases; the process was therefore confounded by everyone without anyone understanding why.

Finally, people acting according to the virtue ethics model are interdependent with their communities' values, mores, and sensibilities. The Breakstone committee was completely separate from its community, focusing little on shared ideals and more on its own interests. The committee's final proposals need not reflect the community's values exactly. In fact, the committee's work may propose a redefinition of community mores or sensibilities to a more ethical or virtuous standard. But working without regard for community standards and values almost assured that the committee's proposals would neither be understood nor supported by the college community. The ideas and suggestions proposed by the committee were admirable and may help bring more students of color into Breakstone and help create an accepting and positive campus climate. But they were not developed comprehensively, nor in a manner likely to result in institutional transformation.

It is not uncommon for institutions to assume that affirmative action in hiring or admissions is incompatible with quality in these areas. Affirmative action is occasionally considered equivalent to lowering quality standards in admissions, hiring, and educational experiences in the classroom. This is a misrepresentation. Affirmative action is designed to maintain or improve quality by ensuring that excellent professionals and students with high academic potential are not excluded because of race, ethnicity, gender, disability, or socioeconomic status. It also ensures that the experiences students have in the classroom and elsewhere on campus will prepare them for their futures in a diverse world where interactions between people of different races, cultures, and sexual orientation are increasing exponentially and can no longer be avoided. Charles Young, the chancellor of the University of California, Los Angeles, said at the 1996 annual meeting of the American Council on Education that the quality of education at UCLA was significantly better than it was twenty-five years before, not in spite of affirmative action, but because of it and the diverse student body it has brought to the institution. Attending a university with a diverse student body and a diversified professional staff helps students learn how to interact with people who see the world through very different lenses and to develop productive professional and personal relationships with them. If the university helps students learn the necessary skills and values, the experience is even more educational than if this learning is left to occur naturally (Fried, 1995).

The Breakstone State committee should have discussed a few basic questions about affirmative action in its deliberations—questions that are seldom asked in the bounds of civil discourse, such as the following:

What are the purposes and intended outcomes of affirmative action?
When you are presented with the terms *affirmative action* and *quality*, what is your reaction?
What has been the impact of affirmative action on your life? Has it been generally positive or generally negative?
What has been the impact of affirmative action on your relationships with students? With faculty? With staff?
What has been the impact of affirmative action on the campus community in general?
How can the success or failure of affirmative action efforts in admission and hiring be measured? Is it solely through the use of numbers, or can qualitative measures about campus atmosphere and the learning environment be part of the evaluation criteria?
Is there still a need for affirmative action? If there is, how might the need be different today than it was ten years ago? If there is no longer a need for affirmative action, how can that be verified?
If you were to design an affirmative action system today with no restrictions, what would it look like?

These questions serve a number of purposes. First, they encourage committee members to confront their own values about affirmative action. Second, they encourage committee members to recognize the impact of affirmative action on themselves, on others, and on their relationships with others, and the impact of affirmative action on their perception of the campus community. Third, answering the questions requires creativity and "out of the box" thinking by committee members. The questions also challenge the belief that affirmative action and quality cannot coexist. But it does not do so by ignoring the legitimate concerns of faculty members about maintaining or improving quality in the classrooms or about instances when poorly qualified people are hired. The hiring of unqualified people is indefensible. But how we define qualifications, and how we determine the skills and perspectives we hope faculty and staff members will bring to the institution, are legitimate questions to explore in discussions of affirmative action and hiring. In short, by infusing consideration of individual and group values, community, and institutional integrity into discussions about affirmative action, the questions require committee members to view affirmative action with a comprehensive ethical perspective.

In the final report, the campus community would have been well served by a brief summary of the committee's discussion of these questions. The relationship between increasing diversity on a campus via affirmative action hiring and enrollment and maintaining quality of educational programs is extremely complex. Published reports often convey a sense of clarity and finality about their recommendations. If the recommendations were preceded by a summary of the committee's conversations, the larger community would begin to realize how ambiguous and difficult the problems are. The committee might wish to suggest further and broader discussions among many members of the campus community in order to continue addressing diversity issues and improving conditions on campus. All the quality management approaches require continuous dialogue for purposes of quality improvement. This report might become a tool to shape immediate changes and future directions, even as it expanded the conversation among all the people who were concerned about the subject.

Free Speech: Another Difficult Case. Perhaps no issue on our campuses is more difficult to talk about than free speech. This is not surprising in a society in which protected speech is often defined as controversial speech that agrees with "my" position, and unprotected or hate speech is defined as controversial speech that attacks "me" or "my" position. Many institutions have tried over the years to develop speech codes that will preserve the basic rights of people to express themselves while also preserving campus environments in which the least powerful can feel comfortable and belong. These codes have generally been found to be unconstitutional. The question remains: How might a college or university develop and nurture an open and accepting community while preserving the rights of community members to disagree on substantive issues?

Many colleges that try to write speech codes or address the issue of free speech do so in response to a crisis. Common examples are skinhead groups plastering a campus with anti-black literature, student groups that sponsor controversial speakers, or faculty members being challenged in court for their classroom behavior. Institutions that try to develop new standards of behavior in response to such incidents will have a difficult time. For one thing, the people who have been offended by the speech will be looking for a quick response to their complaints from administration. When such a solution is forthcoming, it is often cosmetic and fails to confront the antecedents of the behavior. But colleges and universities can seldom choose when such issues arise. What are some effective ways free speech can be addressed on campus?

Take, for example, the situation of the faculty member who uses frequent sexual references in class, making the classroom an uncomfortable environment for women. Commonly, offended students might approach the department chair or dean to protest the instructor's behavior. If approached by the chair or dean, the faculty member might change his behavior, or he might plead "academic freedom" and suggest the dean keep out of his classroom. Alternatively, some students are going to court to challenge what is being said in classrooms, since college and university disciplinary systems seldom regulate faculty classroom behavior. But in many cases, before any substantive action can be taken by the institution, other students may protest the faculty member's attacks on women students. Later, some faculty and staff join the chorus, and within weeks the outside press knocks on the president's door and asks what is being done about the "sexual harassment" in the English department. Such was the case at Pillar University.

President Gould, having completed a successful seven-year tenure as president of Breakstone State College, has returned to her alma mater, Pillar University, an independent institution, to serve as its chief executive. President Gould learned a great deal from her experience at Breakstone, and she decided to involve herself personally in the discussions about free speech.

The president held a campus meeting to express her concern about the tone of discourse on campus, and she stated clearly that she believed there was room in the university community for people with many different views of the world and for forums in which people should be free to express themselves. But, she emphasized, there was no place for directly harassing behavior, nor should people feel threatened because of the speech or behavior of others. She announced the formation of a task force to examine free speech on campus and define what free speech meant to the university community. She asked all members of the university community to participate in any assessment exercises developed by the task force. Finally, she noted that the task force would have until the end of the academic year to complete its work.

The president formed her task force with people from all segments of the institution. She included a faculty member well known for her strong defense of academic freedom as well as the director of the women's center. When the task force was completed, it contained many pairs of people who had spent more time arguing with one another than working toward common goals.

Some people in the university community believed the process was doomed from the start, and privately advised the president to remove some of the more "hard-headed" task force members. She declined.

President Gould first reviewed the remarks from her campus meeting and assured the task force that she was aware that some members of the task force had not worked together in the past, but she hoped they would do so now. She emphasized the difficulty of talking about campus speech without also talking about academic freedom, what it means, why it is valued, and what its place should be in the future. She also talked about the basic mission and goals of the institution, and the part that free speech plays in academic discourse. "If we value academic freedom," she asked, "academic freedom for whom and to what end?"

After assuring herself that the task force understood the basic mission and goals of Pillar, and what its task was to be, the president presented it with a series of questions that she wanted them to answer. These questions were designed to challenge many of their basic notions about speech and discourse on the campus.

What is the role of disagreement in the learning process?

What is academic freedom? What is its purpose? Whom does it protect? How does it help create the learning environment as defined in our institutional mission?

What kind of speech should be protected? Why?

What kind of speech should not be protected. Why?

How do you determine the difference between protected and unprotected-protected speech?

Have you ever been offended or hurt by something someone else said at the university? If so, was the "offending" speech directed at you or at a class of individuals, such as all Jewish people or all black people? In what ways was the "offending" speech congruent with the University's mission?

Have you ever hurt or offended someone or a class of people by something you said while at the university? If so, what do you believe was the impact of your speech on that person or class of people? How do you believe what you said was congruent with the university's mission?

When "offending" speech is directed at individuals or a class of individuals, how does that effect the atmosphere on campus?

When should offending speech not be permitted at the university? Who or what agency should determine what offending speech should not be permitted? Is such a stance in keeping with our mission? What should our community standards for speech be?

If the university should not permit some types of offending speech, how should offenders be disciplined? What mechanisms should be employed?

If the university does not prohibit any types of offending speech, what will be the impact on the university community, and on community members? Is such a stance in keeping with our mission?

During her discussion with the task force, President Gould made clear her expectation that the task force would solicit input from the entire university community so they knew the values and sensibilities of the community. She also asked task force members to acknowledge their own personal biases and to visualize and work toward an ideal university community. In addition, she pledged to meet with the task force chair or entire task force at least monthly to offer her support, suggestions, and assistance.

The president also acknowledged the reluctance of faculty and staff members to enter into a prestructured process but emphasized that the task force's recommendations would need to be acceptable to the entire university community. In addition, she told the task force that the change process they employed must permit them and the university to confront its disagreements and prejudices. With that, she left the room, asking the task force to report back to her the next day outlining the support they believed they would need to complete the task.

President Gould designed a strategy that is likely to succeed. She first focused the task force on the mission, vision, and goals of the institution, in an attempt to ground them in the structure, mores, and sensibilities that undergird all work at the university. This prevented the task force from losing focus. Second, she made it clear that she was going to provide input and guidance but that she expected the task force to come up with a plan that would be acceptable to all and reflect Pillar's principles. She met regularly with the chairs of the task force.

President Gould also began by assuring task force members that she believed they were all motivated to do what is good, though she also acknowledged that they needed to confront their own biases and preconceived notions (Meara, Schmidt, and Day, 1996) about free speech if they were to reach a proper solution. In addition, the time she spent during their first meeting and throughout the change process should provide the training that is frequently absent when institutions undergo change. Also, the questions she posed to the task force and asked them to pose to the university community provided a framework for discussion that addressed the institution's mission, goals, and objectives. They also challenged long-held notions about academic freedom and speech and recognized the importance of considering systems and relationships within the university community when working for systemic change. And she encouraged the task force to ensure congruency of its recommendations with the university's mission. Perhaps most important, though, the president exemplified the virtuous agent by asking the task force members to go beyond the obligations of the university regarding free speech. Instead, she asked them to first determine a higher ideal and then move the university toward it. The president provided a framework that, if followed correctly, should ensure an ethical outcome resulting in long-term, systemic change.

A Case in Progress. Sleepy Hollow College has recently selected its fourteenth president, Dr. Ted Martin. During his interview, Dr. Martin heard about a major reorganization that had taken place under the interim president. He was puzzled by this unusual situation. During the summer he spent two weeks at Sleepy Hollow College in order to initiate some organizational changes and to make contacts with key campus and community members. Dr. Martin believed that a student-centered focus was critical to administration of a college. He thought that relieving the residence life staff of the maintenance functions would allow for more time to be devoted to students and their needs. He initiated discussions of this possible plan. He also toured all the residence halls and discovered that the budget crisis of the past nine years had taken its toll on the facilities. In discussions with senior student affairs administrators, he realized that there was enthusiastic commitment to the program but frustration with the lack of resources to meet the obvious needs. He continued to be puzzled by the incongruities between what he saw in the facilities and what he heard from the staff.

During his interview he had been escorted by Hal Green, the director of physical plant, who was extremely helpful during his stay. The interim president had expressed a great deal of support for Hal and his abilities. On the recommendation of the vice president for business affairs, the board of trustees had given Hal a $15,000 raise at the last board meeting of the academic year. Simultaneously, the board denied raises to two student affairs administrators who had been given increased responsibilities with no increased compensation during the same period. The campus also appeared to have plenty of maintenance equipment, and the grounds were beautiful. There was no apparent reason for the poor maintenance in the residence halls.

The arrival of the new president signaled the last hope that serious campus issues would be addressed. Previous efforts to address frustrations in the residence life program had been unsuccessful because of conflicting management philosophies among the various departments responsible for program and maintenance. According to some reports, the former president was unable to manage the conflicts. Many of the administrators who had taken leadership positions in a campuswide effort to address these issues through implementation of TQM felt unsupported and had become alienated. Several senior administrators left in frustration.

Concurrently with the new president's arrival, a decision was made to leave the position of director of alcohol education vacant as part of the strategy to streamline administrative costs. The person leaving the position had been extremely effective in working with students with substance abuse problems and had successfully intervened and had assisted many students in remaining at Sleepy Hollow College. The incongruity between the arrival of a student-centered president and the elimination of a position designed to support at-risk students was apparent. Many staff and faculty members were extremely concerned about the priorities that had emerged over the past six months under the leadership of the interim president, Dr. Carol Armstrong, who seemed to rely heavily on the advice of the vice president for business affairs. She had shifted management of the Student Center Building and the Campus Security Department from the vice president for student affairs to the director of physical plant. This transfer of responsibilities signaled a move away from student-centered management. This move was problematic because the director of physical plant did not communicate with offices in the student affairs division. He often stated that his workload made attending meetings impossible.

The dean of students knew of the many difficulties facing the campus and its staff. Many hours of her day were spent responding to student problems involving the same offices that did not serve students well. She had received reports of problems for many years, and had sent several memos to the previous president outlining the issues and suggesting solutions. Until now those steps had resulted in no change. She was aware through the campus grapevine that efforts to discredit the student affairs division with Dr. Martin were being made behind the scenes. Ethically, she felt impelled to bring the problem to the president's attention. The question she faced was how to do it in a way that would do no harm, benefit the campus community, and be fair to all parties concerned. The president arrives on campus next week to take up his new duties. What should the dean of students do?

Conclusion

In light of the inevitability of change, student affairs practitioners should approach their work in a manner that will prepare them and others for long-lasting, effective change. Such change results primarily from challenging the assumptions on which student development work is based. If it is true that the structure and systems of American higher education are inadequate for the challenges of the future, then what is needed are different paradigms for student affairs and higher education in general. These can only be developed by challenging existing paradigms and systems, reaffirming basic values, and working to create systems and relationships that support student development work. This comprehensive approach to decision making and processes should ensure consideration of ethical concerns as well.

Student affairs colleagues should be reminded frequently of the mission and goals of the institution. These should be communicated to students and faculty as well. Student affairs staff members should be encouraged to remember the importance of systems and relationships in their work and be reminded that these systems and relationships have as much to do with division success in teaching students as any theoretical construct or pedagogy.

Many people in colleges and universities resist change, partly because it has hurt them in the past. Involving such people in working for positive change is one way of lowering their resistance. And it supports the notion that all members of the college or university community can learn and can contribute to the institution's future.

The process of forming and charging working committees is important and should be approached carefully and deliberately. Committees and working groups should be truly representative of the diversity of the community, not only in numbers by constituency, but in belief systems, values, and perspectives. It does nothing to create a task force to look at free speech that contains only those people who have been offended by someone else's speech or only those who advocate a complete hands-off approach to discourse by faculty. Building committees in this manner should have long-lasting positive effects on the campus community, even though the committees may spin their wheels before resolving conflicts about perspectives and biases.

Departments of student affairs should be encouraged to form advisory committees of staff members, students, and faculty. The committees should review the missions, goals, and objectives of the department and help the department head by providing feedback and advice throughout the year. Too often student affairs departments review basic documents and procedures every few years but seldom ask the customers, or primary constituents and others, how they are doing and whether what they are doing makes a difference in the lives of the constituents.

One of the systems in higher education that tends to be broken more than it works is the system of communication and work among faculty members and student affairs practitioners. When this system does not work, the ultimate losers are students. Building bridges and relationships with faculty members—that is, creating new systems involving faculty and student development practitioners—must be a high priority if the goal of serving students better is to be reached.

Student affairs practitioners can and should be the conscience of their campuses. They should remind other administrators and faculty of why the institution exists—its purpose, its mission. Pointing out to them conflicts between what the institution says it stands for and what it does is a valuable and necessary function. By serving this role, student affairs will help colleges and universities remain places of ethical teaching and learning.

References

Cause. "Challenges and Opportunities of Information Technology in the 90s." In *Proceedings of the Cause National Conference*. Boulder, Colo.: CAUSE, 1991.

Childress, J., and Senn, L. *In the Eye of the Storm: Reengineering Corporate Culture*. Los Angeles: The Leadership Press, 1995.

Cornesky, R., and McCool, S. *Total Quality Improvement Guide for Institutions of Higher Education*. Madison, Wis.: Magna Publications, 1992.

Cornesky, R., McCool, S., Byrnes, L., and Weber, R. *Implementing Total Quality Management in Higher Education*. Madison, Wis.: Magna Publications, 1991.

Entin, D. "Whither TQM: A Second Look." *AAHE Bulletin*, 1994, *46*, XX-7.

Fried, J. *Shifting Paradigms in Student Affairs: Culture, Context, Teaching and Learning*. Washington, D.C.: American College Personnel Association, 1995.

Grace, R., and Templin, T. "QSS: Quality Student Services." *NASPA Journal*, 1994, *32*, 74–80.

Kitchener, K. "Ethical Principles and Ethical Decisions in Student Affairs." In H. J. Canon and R. D. Brown (eds.), *Applied Ethics in Student Services*. New Directions for Student Services, no. 30. San Francisco: Jossey-Bass, 1985.

Meara, N., Schmidt, L., and Day, J. "Principles and Virtues: A Foundation for Ethical Decisions, Policies and Character." *The Counseling Psychologist,* 1996, 24 (1), 4–77.

Penrod, J., and Dolence, M. *Reengineering: A Process for Transforming Higher Education.* Professional Paper series, no. 9. Boulder, Colo.: CAUSE, 1992.

Rion, M. *The Responsible Manager.* Amherst, Mass.: Human Resource Development Press, 1989.

Schön, D. A. *Educating the Reflective Practitioner: Toward a New Design for Teaching and Learning in the Professions.* San Francisco: Jossey-Bass, 1990.

Senge, P. M. *The Fifth Discipline.* New York: Doubleday, 1990.

Speck, S. "Balancing Cost and Quality: Case Studies in Determining Tuition at Independent Colleges and Universities." Paper presented at the annual Meeting of National Association for Independent Colleges and Universities, Washington, D.C., 1996.

F. J. TALLEY is vice president for student affairs and dean of students at Bryant College and a member of the Ethics Committee of the American College Personnel Association.

This chapter suggests innovative approaches to enhancing dialogue about institutional purpose and competition for limited resources between faculty members and student affairs staff in order to increase understanding and mutual respect in times of conflict.

Ethical Dialogues on Campus

David Carl Sundberg, Jane Fried

Faculty of the future must be able to facilitate student learning beyond the classroom, become involved in multidisciplinary activities, and engage with external constituencies (Buchen, 1987). As faculty become involved with student learning beyond the classroom, it seems appropriate for student affairs professionals to work with students in a manner that enhances classroom learning. Holistic learning, usually a responsibility of student affairs professionals, is becoming integrated with academic learning. Despite changing approaches to teaching and learning, faculty members and student affairs professionals continue to experience difficulty in engaging a dialogue about the purposes of higher education or collaborating effectively in transcending the traditional dichotomies of living and learning. They continue to be "bowling alone" (Edgerton, 1995) despite their responsibility to prepare students for global interdependence and increasing collaboration in all phases of their personal and professional lives. Discussions of the various ethical approaches that student affairs professionals and faculty members use to make decisions; develop curricula and educational programs; and allocate time, money, and other resources can provide a good starting place for campus dialogues about our common educational purposes, because our ethical frameworks govern our choices in all these areas.

Extending Traditional Models

Kitchener (1985) reminds us that making ethical choices and thinking through ethical issues are at the very core of our work as student affairs professionals. The foundation of ethical thought and behavior rests on our ability to determine "what acts or behaviors are 'right' or 'ought to be done/not done' as well as determining the epistemological justifications for ethical statements or assertions"

(Winston and Saunders, 1991, p. 331). In a pluralistic and diverse society, professional responsibilities are becoming increasingly complex. The dual duties of helping the individual and promoting the good of society now must be seen from an increasing variety of perspectives, including those shaped by culture, profession, and institutional role. To meet these dual expectations, professionals must be able to compare the value and effectiveness of multiple ethical models in complex situations on college campuses. We must also be able to interpret the language of ethical decision making to people who are affected by decisions, to translate ethical theories into informed practice, and to create an ethical decision-making process that can be adapted to many situations.

Kitchener (1984, 1985) has stated that ethical decision making is a matter of set and setting and that a professional has a responsibility to examine the facts of a situation before deciding which ethical rules, principles, and theories might be applied. She proposes "three increasingly general and more abstract levels of ethical reasoning" and suggests that "appeals can be made to a higher level if a lower, more specific level fails to provide the rationale for a decision" (Kitchener, 1985, p. 18). The first level is that of ethical rules that could "function somewhat like a set of laws for [an] organization" (p. 19). The next level of reasoning, ethical principles, can help a practitioner "provide a level of justification when ethical codes are silent or ambiguous" (p. 19). Kitchener does not engage in analysis of the third level of ethical theory. She states that when one "must decide between moral principles, [one] should decide in a way that is consistent with what [one] would want for [one's self], [one's] loved ones and all others under the same circumstances" (p. 28). How broadly one defines *all others* is a crucial issue. There has been too little dialogue about the process of creating ethical communities on campus and determining who the others are when ethical choices are being made. In all cases, the predominant principle is doing no harm or doing as little harm as possible.

Traditionally, ethical decision making has been based on rational principles (Fried, Chapter One of this volume; Fried, 1995) with little emphasis placed on the role of intuition or feeling in this process. By adding consideration of feeling and intuition, as has been done in many relational ethical systems (Alcoff, 1988; Rhoads and Black, 1995), it is possible to expand one's understanding of doing harm by combining the notion of doing right according to principle with doing good, taking feelings and an intuitive sense of well-being into account. Approaching events from a broader base of understanding creates a greater sense of commonality and responsibility for personal and collective behavior and outcomes.

Barriers to Change. Factionalism and fractionalizing among departments on campuses has made professional conversations among faculty in the same departments difficult and has rendered professional conversations between student affairs professionals and faculty even more difficult. Specialization, which has increased depth of understanding in one area, has often rendered specialized knowledge too narrow to be useful in another area. Generalists in any area have the opposite problem, too much breadth and too little depth in any particular area of expertise. As a consequence, there seems to be a tendency on the part of people in both groups to trivialize the contributions of others and to marginalize them as participating colleagues in campus decisions. Feelings of marginalization limit participation in the community and contribute to increasing alienation (Schlossberg, 1989) and lack of dialogue about ethics or any other topic of common concern.

Other barriers to change include the widely held belief that divisions between faculty and student affairs staff are somehow natural, with faculty on the intellectual side of the chasm and student affairs on the other side, which is far less well defined but includes all of student life. Fear of the Other, protection of role, anxiety about not being able to meet new expectations, unwillingness to risk failure, and inability to cross borders also contribute to maintaining the status quo. On the other hand, the desire to enhance student learning, increasing public expectations about higher education, and the excitement of rethinking learning encounters can provide a powerful impetus for renewed conversations about the goals and purposes of campus communities. An excellent starting point in building relationships and stimulating dialogue is in discussion of ethical concerns about behavior, resource allocation, restructuring, and externally imposed demands for change in governance, pedagogy, and management. Indeed, any discussion of these topics could begin with a discussion of the assumptions and beliefs about "the good" that shape the contributions of discussants (See Talley, Chapter Three of this volume).

Differences in Faculty and Student Affairs Perspectives on Ethics. There is a sense of bewilderment among staff and faculty about what to make of the modern college student. The phrase *make of* has several connotations, including *how to understand* and *what ought we turn them into*. The ways in which students costume themselves, use language, see themselves as responsible, and establish priorities for use of time and other resources can be very confusing to nonstudent observers. Adding to this confusion is additional confusion about staff and faculty responsibilities in relating to these students and student status with regard to legal adulthood and personal competence. The age of majority is eighteen in cases of voting rights, but various legal rights of adulthood may be granted as early as sixteen in cases of suspected addiction or pregnancy or as late as twenty-one where certain financial or contractual rights are concerned. The principle approach of establishing a universal rule, such as age, tends to prevail over the virtues approach of evaluating adulthood in terms of ability to engage in responsible or prudent behavior in the context of a particular community. These conflicting sets of ideas make a consistent institutional approach to student behavior or student learning almost impossible. In addition, the distinction between living and learning that exists in the minds of many faculty members and student affairs professionals as well as in the policies and architecture of many colleges and universities compounds the difficulty. What is a faculty member's responsibility for student problems and preoccupations, particularly when it is obvious that a student's preoccupation is interfering with the academic learning process? What is a student affairs staff member's responsibility for learning if she or he realizes that the student's main learning emphasis is on finding out how to download prewritten term papers from Internet resources? Consensus about what a college-educated person ought to look like, know, or be able to do upon graduating has evaporated. Questions about who is responsible for the development of the intellect or development of the character are again being raised. There are descriptions of the educated person (Hall and Kevles, 1982) but there seems to be little consensus about responsibility for creating the environment in which a person can become educated and develop intellectually or emotionally.

Many faculty still assume that responsibility for student life belongs to student affairs, and many student affairs professionals assume that teaching and intellectual development are the sole responsibility of the faculty. Courses in ethics tend to engage the students intellectually and present multiple ideas about ethical approaches. They tend not to address the process by which a student makes sense of his or her emotional reactions to the conflicts that different systems create for her or him. In contrast, numerous areas of student life, such as student activities and programming, career planning, residence life, and community service present opportunities for discussion of ethical issues, but the intellectual tradition of ethical inquiry tends to receive little attention. Little exploration has been done to determine if this traditional division of effort is still appropriate. On campuses where community service has become community service learning, the division is beginning to disappear (see Saltmarsh, Chapter Five of this volume). Examination of the case studies presented later in this chapter presents an approach to opening a dialogue about responsibility, ethics, and the evolution of common educational purpose.

Considerations in Addressing Ethical Dilemmas. Hoekema (1990) has described three conditions necessary for making moral and ethical decisions. The first is that responsible choices can only be made when the chooser is aware of a range of options. A mature moral decision is an informed decision. The second is that moral maturity entails giving weight to the ethical view of others without letting those views function as a substitute for one's own considered judgment. The process of making choices involves balancing and evaluating contrasting points of view. Finally, mature moral decisions are made in the awareness of consequences. Moral choices involve consideration of potential outcomes and a willingness to take responsibility for the consequences. Morally mature individuals may disagree about the best choice but each is prepared to make a choice and stand by it. One way to untangle conflicting claims would be to apply Hoekema's conditions to each argument and initiate a dialogue that might lead to a satisfactory outcome and increased understanding.

A Matrix of Principles and Evolving Roles

The roles suggested in this section have evolved without reference to job description or official organizational function. They are interpreter-linguist, translator, transformational architect, and reflective practitioner. The *interpreter-linguist* attends to the differing use of language across groups, including formal, idiomatic, and nonverbal language. In a dialogue where participants seem to misunderstand each other consistently, the interpreter-linguist can move beyond her or his institutional role as, for example, a member of the sociology or English department, to her functional role, using her academic training and observation skills to help individuals understand each other. Dialogue often strengthens community and increases people's ability to understand each other's perspectives even when they do not agree. Real dialogue increases feelings of mutual acceptance, respect, and understanding and decreases feelings of exclusion or marginalization. Continuing dialogue enhances toleration (Strike and Soltis, 1992).

The *translator* is skilled at applying theory to practice and helping people see or experience the world from multiple perspectives. Boal's "Joker" (1992) is an example of the translator role in action. The Joker in the Theater of the Oppressed helps participants gather their thoughts, prepare their actions, imagine potential outcomes, and replay possible outcomes if the anticipated consequences are undesirable. Jokers decide nothing and impose no viewpoint but act as midwives to the birth of a mutually acceptable approach to addressing a dilemma. This is an essential role in facilitating dialogue between faculty and student affairs staff and between people who have a long-range view of events and those whose perspectives are limited by their own anticipated involvement. The short-term perspective tends to be used by students, because they typically matriculate for a specific, limited period of time. Jokers keep the dialogue going, not by making jokes but by challenging assumptions and keeping all the possibilities open. Anyone with imagination, a disengaged perspective, and an ability to keep community welfare in mind can play this role. The role is different from the devil's advocate because the devil's advocate is oppositional by nature. The Joker is exploratory and expands the range of possibilities.

The *transformational architect* uses space and physical environments to transform relationships. She or he may begin with an awareness of campus ecology (Banning, 1989) or program planning models that take person-environment interaction into account (Aulepp and Delworth, 1976; Huebner and Corazzini, 1978). This role involves attention to the interaction between people and their environment, a sensitivity to the effects that environmental arrangements have on communication, and a willingness to bring these issues to discussion as appropriate. The visual anthropology discussed by Banning in Chapter Six of this volume presents some of the data a transformational architect might use to support rearrangement of physical space to enhance human interaction. The role of transformational architect directly supports Crookston's early definition of education for human development, "the creation of a human learning environment within which individuals, teachers and social systems interact and utilize developmental tasks for personal growth and social betterment" (1973, p. 57). A person in this role views the entire environment as a teaching or learning tool. She or he analyzes the messages inherent in the environment and tries to make them consistent with the espoused values of the university.

The role of *reflective practitioner* was described by Schön (1983, 1990) as he mapped the work environments of professionals in a fast-changing, pragmatic world. Schön consistently reminds professionals in all fields of the need to maintain an internal dialogue between the consistencies of theory and the vagaries of practice. A reflective practitioner does not apply theory to practice. He or she engages in a reflective analysis of the relationship between the two so that practice improves and theory evolves to cover more of the specifics that constitute practice. Everyone on campus can become a reflective practitioner by sharing their internal dialogues about discrepancies between their ideals and ethical beliefs and the realities of campus problems that must be addressed. Rather than hiding concerns about the inevitable inconsistencies between theory and practice, open conversation normalizes ongoing inquiry and community concern with ethical decision making. Improvement can be made by engaging in theory-to-practice dialogue as part of the decision-making, implementation, and review process. Ethical conversation requires reflection. Reflection requires knowledge of one's own ideas about community welfare and the purposes of the enterprise. It also requires a type of detachment: the ability to express one's own beliefs and listen open-mindedly to others who are equally committed to their beliefs without becoming defensive.

Table 4.1 maps a matrix of interaction between roles and principles. The reader is invited to construct additional matrices that shape thinking about

Table 4.1. Interaction Between Roles and Principles

Evolving Roles	Respecting autonomy	Doing no harm	Benefiting others	Being just	Being faithful
Interpreter-linguist	Listens carefully to the language of the speaker and interprets it accurately, avoiding imposing his or her own meanings. Attends carefully to denotative, connotative meanings, including those from the affective domain.	Avoids, by use of inflection, gesture, or other behavior, degrading the message being interpreted or the messenger.	Makes sure that all participants have reasonably and accurately been provided an opportunity to decode and encode messages being sent from one to the other, including messages that have emotional importance. Is comfortable working with affect.	Carefully studies and understands all the dialects being used in communications between and among individuals and makes sure that each receives equal attention in both detail and consideration.	Makes known to all parties the guidelines by which he or she functions, the limits of her or his expertise, and does not go beyond these. Remains true to the principles that guide the practice of being an interpreter linguist and removes self from setting if unable to act in good faith.
Translator	Helps all parties discover the implications of moving from theory to practice both in short-term and long-term	Indicates possible negative consequences of decisions or actions for all participants. Takes the nec-	Ensures that all those who wish to examine the effects of decisions are given ample opportunity to do so.	Examines the implications for distribution of resources in terms of equity, opportunity, and fair-	Understands and ascertains that all parties understand the purposes for which decisions are being made,

Evolving Roles	Respecting autonomy	Doing no harm	Benefiting others	Being just	Being faithful
Translator (continued)	costs and outcomes. May assist in clarifying issues, but ought not impose her or his own agenda on the process.	essary time and is persistent in insisting that issues be examined in sufficient depth.	Helps those who are silenced to be heard. Helps the less articulate or forceful to express their ideas, feelings, and concerns.	ness as an idea, theory, or plan is implemented. Seeks to ensure an equitable distribution of resources and that all parties have reasonable opportunity to benefit from the decisions made.	the mission and goals that all have agreed to follow. Behaves in ways consistent with these as well as directing all parties to be equally consistent.
Transformational architect	Ensures that the physical and psychological environments in which decisions are made are conducive to open, honest discussion and decision making and that no party is made to feel threatened in his or her discussion of issues or in expressing feelings or ideas.	Does not try to force a decision on a participant or allow undue pressure to be brought by other stakeholders on individuals who have differing ideas or opinions.	Helps redesign environments that are not conducive to free and open discussion or that are oppressive to individuals engaged in the decision-making process. Makes others aware of how their behavior may contribute to an oppressive environment and helps them make necessary adaptations.	Gives equal attention to attempts to unduly influence or pressure individuals on the part of all participants. Insists that the guidelines established apply equally to all and that any reconstruction of the physical or psychological environments are made so that all benefit.	Attends carefully to such environmental decisions as how allocations of resources, including space, budgets and other forms of support, are made. Requests that all decisions demonstrably contribute to the mission and goals of the institution and are not made arbitrarily or on the basis of lesser ends.
Reflective practitioner	Takes time to comprehend how each party might define autonomy and works toward consensus in defining the optimum level of autonomy versus interdependence as the decision-making process unfolds. Is aware of social and cultural differences among members of the group and how such differences affect the thinking and feeling states of each participant and may diminish her or his ability to express needs and ideas.	Takes time to examine possible harmful outcomes for alternate plans being studied and makes these known to all participants.	Helps all parties explore ways in which compromise and collaboration can be used to arrive at optimum benefits to all and makes sure that the conditions of any compromise are met.	Seeks to understand how diverse members of the community understand the concepts of justice, fairness, and equitable treatment and helps all parties see each others' points of view. Helps all parties achieve consensus about being just and being fair.	Actively and intentionally develops the skills, knowledge, and practices of a reflective practitioner and is open and honest about where such reflection leads, not possessive of ideas and discoveries.

ethically sound thinking and behavior in dialogues where several types of ethical principles, organizational roles, community virtues, or long-standing relationships intersect.

Cases and Discussion

The well-meaning professor. A professor becomes aware that about one-third of the students in his class are from migrant worker families. He discovers that these students are not as well prepared as other students and wishes to see them succeed in his class. In his evaluation of their work, the professor uses criteria that are less rigorous and demanding than those used for other students. Students in the class discover this practice. Initially some of the migrant students feel a sense of relief. They feel they have a better chance of succeeding. Other students are resentful of the different grading practices. After a while some of the migrant worker students begin to think that they are being let down, particularly when they discover they will still be competing for jobs with students who have been evaluated according to higher standards. Students from both sides complain to the provost and to the vice-president for student life. There is much discussion of equity, of accommodation of diverse students, and of the ethics of the professor's choice to use different standards for the two groups.

There are several principles in conflict in this situation-fairness in grading standards; the harm done to the migrant students by providing them with a less demanding level of education, which will further disadvantage them in competition for jobs; the belief that all students, given the opportunity, are capable of learning what the course description states that they can learn. The roles of interpreter-linguist, translator, and reflective practitioner can all play a part in addressing the situation. Although the professor is well intentioned, he may not understand how his behavior looks to either group of students. The relationships of many people are at risk in this situation and the environment created by the professor is sending a confusing and aggravating message to students and faculty alike.

What approach might the provost and vice-president for student life design to yield a satisfactory, ethically justifiable resolution? There may be no right answer to the question of how to educate underprepared students. There may be many answers that different groups of people consider right. One effective way to determine a satisfactory approach is to map the issues on a set of matrices created for the purpose of identifying the issues and their relative importance to all parties concerned, to present the map to the individuals involved, and to begin a dialogue. Solutions to this problem based on ethical principles imposed on the situation without reference to the competing ethical perspectives and relationships among members of the class and the campus community are bound to be unsatisfactory. Although the principles remain constant, the realities of each community vary and must be respected. Process, mutual respect, and ongoing dialogue must govern eventual outcomes.

The bulletin board abuser. (Leo, 1996). A student was seen by a professor in the act of tearing down a flier from a bulletin board. The professor saw the act as censorship. The student saw herself as having the right to tear down anything she did not like. The professor was a white male and the student a female of "mixed ancestry" (Leo, 1996, p. 22). The perspectives that present themselves are those of the author of the column, the student, the professor, other faculty, and various university administrators, as well as readers of the article.

Ethical role and principle matrices developed by student affairs professionals (Brown and Krager, 1985; Krager, 1985) are useful in this case as well. In an age when physicists and philosophers are hypothesizing the existence of ten dimensions in their search for a "theory of everything" (Hawking and Penrose, 1996), it may be archaic to pursue solutions from a two-dimensional framework. Using these matrices in a two-dimensional manner with little reflection about the effects of subsequent decisions on the overall campus climate or the long-range implications for individuals is inadequate. Two- or three- dimensional matrices, such as the one presented by Banning in Chapter Six of this volume, must be used as a guide to decision making rather than a cross-tabulation that points to "right" answers. A metaperspective that invites a more reflective, holistic, and less role- and ego-bound process may provide greater insight.

As one examines the bulletin board abuser case, several roles and ethical principles become apparent. The student has observed offensive material and is, in her view, justified in removing it from public view. This may be interpreted by her as preventing harm to others. She is acting autonomously and spontaneously in a manner that is somewhat unusual for women (Rich, 1986) and is expressing her opinion in a manner that seems entirely reasonable to her. The professor who observed her action has another perspective. He sees the student's action as one of property destruction and denial of freedom of speech that is harmful to the tradition of open expression that is a core campus value.

The campus had no resolution process for addressing these types of conflicts. The process created to address the situation failed to honor due process or ethical principles. The professor was admonished for "verbally abusing" the student. The administrative stance was presented as neutral. "We have no position on putting things up on bulletin boards or taking things down" (Leo, 1996, p. 22). This can be seen as an instance in which meaningful dialogue across borders was not encouraged. Unfortunately, "such crossings are often ignored or suppressed . . . [if] they can be disruptive or embarrassing to the institution or department" (Fried, 1995, p.92). Administrative expediency is often chosen over educational engagement in potentially difficult circumstances.

Consolidating cultural programs. A large university has supported several cultural studies programs for the past fifteen years—the Latino Studies program, the African American Studies program, the Women's Studies program, and the Islamic Studies program. Each of these programs offers academic majors and minors and acts as a cultural center and gathering place for students who identify with the area of study. Each also has an advisory board composed of students, faculty members, and community representatives. The programs have historically received different levels of financial support from the university and community, have provided different types of services to students, and have each had their own director, secretary, and office suite. When the university suffered a drastic decline in enrollment, budgets were reviewed. The review committee suggested that all these programs be consolidated into a Cultural Studies department. The department would have a single chair and two secretaries. The consolidated budget was cut by 50 percent and allocated to the department as a whole. The department would occupy a building on the edge of campus that had almost as much space as all the programs had occupied previously, but was on a side street, far from the academic center of the campus. Each individual program would be administered by a graduate student under the supervision of the chair. No members of these programs were on the review committee, nor were opinions of program participants solicited before the review committee made its recommendation.

As soon as the consolidation became public, an uproar began. Faculty members were furious about the anticipated cut in the number of courses. Students from the different groups had previously had little interaction and had very different ideas about how to use the space. Social norms varied drastically between groups. Two secretaries and three administrators were about to lose their jobs, and services to students in all groups were about to be cut. In addition, members of all constituent communities in the city immediately became aware of the cuts, were angry because their options had not been solicited, and began to lose confidence in the university's frequent public statements about serving the needs of various ethnic groups in the city.

The ethical issues in this case are extremely complex. The first issue is the method by which the recommendation was determined. F. J. Talley, in Chapter Three of this volume, describes the consequences of making decisions on emotionally loaded issues without input from those most directly affected and without the support of the chief decision makers who have fiduciary responsibility for total institutional welfare. The decision-making process exhibited neither adherence to principles nor acknowledgment of virtues. The university had supported these programs as separate entities for more than a decade; therefore, deciding to combine them and cut their collective budgets was neither prudent, respectful, nor benevolent. The recommendation lacked integrity in the most profound sense because it broke up four programs with four different cultural perspectives and combined them into one. The new program represented the perspective of the dominant culture: the programs, because they studied and represented nondominant cultures, could collectively be considered The Other. Others, when they become a group, are seen as unified by contrast to the perspective of the dominant group. This approach does not respect the internal perspective of any of the reorganized groups.

The process also violated approaches inherent in relational ethics (Alcoff, 1988; Noddings, 1984). It ignored collaborative relationships that members of these groups might have developed and simultaneously placed all groups in opposition to each other for limited resources. Finally, it left the group members the task of sorting out potential resolutions to the mandate without benefit of an overarching university goal or specific guidance from a high-ranking academic or administrative officer.

The traditional response to this type of dilemma is that the bottom line is the most important factor in any institutional decision making. The bottom line is a code term for financial responsibility and solvency. It is a moving target that represents the consensus among the governing group about values, institutional purposes, and priorities. It is not a naturally existing fact of nature. There are as many ways to maintain a sound financial posture as there are interpretations of institutional values. Institutional willingness to debate various means for retaining financial solvency can be seen as evidence of a commitment to integrating ethics and purpose into the discussion rather than imposing one set of beliefs on all stakeholders in the organization. This type of problem will become increasingly frequent as universities reconfigure their resources, so the most ethical approach is to develop processes, relationships, and consensus to the degree possible about institutional priorities before a crisis mandates that specific decisions be made in a limited period of time. Factionalized, fractionalized universities do not make ethical or effective decisions because of the inability of the conflicting parties to understand or appreciate different perspectives. They cannot achieve the level of moral maturity described by Hoekema (1990) as being well-informed about choices, balancing personal values with understanding of values held by others in the situation, and remaining committed to choices even when consequences are not what one anticipated.

Conclusion

Dialogue is the key word in the process of ethical decision making on campus. In these times of changing national values, changing technologies and research methodologies, and dramatic fluctuations in the international economy, all institutions must assume that change is constant. No ethical system can be assumed to dominate across institutions or across situations. If decision makers assume a consensus about values and ethics in a particular situation, disagreement, alienation, and possibly disruption are almost sure to follow publication of any decision. It is possible for individual campuses to develop systems of ethical priorities and values through extensive dialogue and creation of respectful relationships even among those whose priorities are often in conflict. It is certainly possible to achieve improved communication among groups that have historically been divided from each other to the point where they often misunderstand each other's values and motives. A decision to enhance or even initiate dialogue about ethics and campus values may be seen as a waste of time when issues such as enrollment, solvency, maintenance of the physical plant, expansion of Internet access, and technology acquisition are seen as more pressing.

Initiation of dialogue demonstrates a long-term view of an ongoing process, not a response to an immediate crisis. Hospitals and businesses routinely support ethics committees and offices of corporate responsibility (Rion, 1989). It is not unusual for one person to be employed full-time to review decisions and initiate discussions. Perhaps it is time for universities to adopt a similar approach by designating an ethics officer with staff status who reports directly to the president. Failure to initiate this type of conversation is by far worse than assuming consensus and being forced to deal with the continuous conflict that inevitably follows. Universities of the late twentieth century are attempting to reframe themselves in a world of unprecedented change and interaction. If there is no dialogue across borders, we will continue to find ourselves, in the words of Matthew Arnold, "wandering between two worlds, one dead, the other powerless to be born" (Arnold, [1867] 1962, p. 876).

References

Alcoff, L. "Cultural Feminism Versus Post-Structuralism: The Identity Crisis in Feminist Theory." *Signs,* 1988, *13,* 405–435.

Arnold, M. "Stanzas from the Grande Chartreuse." In M. Abrams (ed.), *The Norton Anthology of English Literature.* Vol. 2. New York: W. W. Norton, 1962. (Originally published 1867.)

Aulepp, L., and Delworth, U. *Training Manual for an Ecosystem Model.* Boulder, Colo.: Western Interstate Commission for Higher Education, 1976.

Banning, J. "Creating a Climate for Successful Student Development: The Campus Ecology Manager Role." In U. Delworth, G. R. Hansen, and Associates, *Student Services: A Handbook for the Profession.* (2nd ed.) San Francisco: Jossey-Bass, 1989.

Boal, A. *Games for Actors and Non-Actors.* New York: Routledge, 1992.

Brown, R., and Krager, L. "Ethical Issues in Graduate Education: Faculty and Student Responsibilities." *Journal of Higher Education,* 1985, *56,* 403–418.

Buchen, I. "Faculty for the Future." *The Futurist,* Nov.-Dec. 1987, *21* (6), 22–27.

Crookston, B. "Education for Human Development." In C. Warnath (ed.), *New Directions for College Counselors.* San Francisco: Jossey-Bass, 1973.

Edgerton, R. "Bowling Alone: An Interview with Robert Putnam About American's Collapsing Civic Life." *AAHE Bulletin,* 1995, *48,* 3–6.

Fried, J. *Shifting Paradigms in Student Affairs: Culture, Context, Teaching and Learning.* Washington, D.C.: American College Personnel Association, 1995.

Hall, J., and Kevles, B. (eds). *In Opposition to Core Curriculum.* Westport, Conn.: Greenwood Press, 1982.

Hawking, S., and Penrose, R. "The Nature of Space and Time." *Scientific American,* 1996, *275* (1), 60–65.

Hoekema, D. "Beyond *in loco parentis*? Parietal Rules and Moral Maturity." In S. Cahn (ed.), *Morality, Responsibility and the University.* Philadelphia: Temple University Press, 1990.

Huebner, L., and Corazzini, J. "Eco-Mapping: A Dynamic Model for Intentional Campus Design." *Journal Supplement Abstract Service.* 1978.

Kitchener, K. "Intuition, Critical Evaluation and Ethical Principles: The Foundation for Ethical Principles in Counseling Psychology." *The Counseling Psychologist,* 1984, *12,* 43–55.

Kitchener, K. "Ethical Principles and Ethical Decisions in Student Affairs." In H. J. Cannon and R. D. Brown (eds.), *Applied Ethics in Student Services*. New Directions for Student Services, no. 30. San Francisco: Jossey-Bass, 1985.

Krager, L. "A New Model for Defining Ethical Behavior." In H. J. Cannon and R. D. Brown (eds.), *Applied Ethics in Student Services*. New Directions for Student Services, no. 30. San Francisco: Jossey-Bass, 1985.

Leo, J. "Abusing Bulletin Boards." *US News and World Report,* Jan. 29, 1996, p. 22.

Noddings, N. *Caring: A Feminine Approach to Ethics and Moral Education*. Berkeley: University of California Press, 1984.

Rhoads, R., and Black, M. "Student Affairs Practitioners as Transformative Educators: Advancing a Critical Cultural Perspective." *Journal of College Student Development,* 1995, 36, 413–421.

Rich, A. *Blood, Bread and Poetry: Selected Prose, 1979-1985*. New York: W. W. Norton, 1986.

Rion, M. *The Responsible Manager*. Amherst, Mass.: Human Resource Development Press, 1989.

Schlossberg, N. "Marginality and Mattering: Key Issues in Building Community." In D. Roberts (ed.), *Designing Campus Activities to Foster a Sense of Community*. New Directions for Student Services, no. 48. San Francisco: Jossey-Bass, 1989.

Schön, D. A. *The Reflective Practitioner*. New York: Basic Books, 1983.

Schön, D. A. *Educating the Reflective Practitioner: Toward a New Design for Teaching and Learning in the Professions*. San Francisco: Jossey-Bass, 1990.

Strike, K., and Soltis, J. *The Ethics of Teaching*. (2nd ed.) New York: Teachers College Press, 1992.

Winston, R., and Saunders, S. "The Greek Experience: Friend or Foe in Student Development." In R. B. Winston, W. R. Nettles III, and J. H. Opper (eds.), *Fraternities and Sororities on the Contemporary College Campus*. New Directions for Student Services, no. 40. San Francisco: Jossey-Bass, 1987.

Winston, R., and Saunders, S. "Ethical Professional Practice in Student Affairs." In T. Miller, R. Winston, and Associates, *Administration and Leadership in Student Affairs*. (2nd ed.) Muncie, Ind.: Accelerated Development, 1991.

DAVID CARL SUNDBERG *is associate professor and coordinator of the College Student Personnel Administration and Higher Education Programs at Central Missouri State University and is chair of the Ethics Committee of the American College Personnel Association.*

JANE FRIED *is associate professor in the Department of Health and Human Services at Central Connecticut State University and is former chair of the Standing Committee on Ethics of the American College Personnel Association.*

By combining service, reflection, and connected, interpersonal learning, students develop an identity that is grounded on mutual responsibility and a personal understanding of democracy.

Ethics, Reflection, Purpose, and Compassion: Community Service Learning

John Saltmarsh

There is a profound transformation unfolding in higher education. The paradigm from which higher education is emerging is one characterized by "separate knowing" (Belenky, Clinchy, Goldberger, and Tarule, 1986), which is based on specialized knowledge and disciplinary categorization of information and ideas. It is presided over by faculty whose authority rests on their superior knowledge, which they impart to receptive students. That authority is exercised in classrooms that center the teacher as the focus of learning, reward retention of abstract information, and legitimize distancing the knower from the construction of knowledge. Values become cognitive constructs rather than personal beliefs, and moral education is based on impersonal standards and procedures for establishing justice. Separate knowing is emphasized in institutions where academic affairs is separate from student affairs, as if the cognitive development of students could be separate from their affective and behavioral growth. In the world of separate knowing, universities are removed from and unrelated to the communities and neighborhoods in which they are located. In a framework of separate knowing, learning is considered the process of depositing information. It happens only in the separate world of the school and is believed to cease with graduation. Life is what comes after education.

The paradigm challenging separate knowing is one characterized by "connected knowing" (Belenky, Clinchy, Goldberger, and Tarule, 1986). The purpose of this chapter is to contrast separate and connected knowing as a means by which to understand the transformations that higher education must undertake to integrate ethics education into both theoretical and applied curricula. Although the pedagogy of separate knowing may teach students how to think about ethical ideas, it does not necessarily teach them how to recognize ethical issues that regularly arise in life or give them the will to make ethical choices. *Service learning* is used as a vehicle to describe one powerful approach to ethics education, using the pedagogy of connected knowing. Connected knowing posits the fundamental centrality of relations in learning and in life as a whole. In this paradigm, education "integrates thought and action, reason and emotion, education and life" and "does not divorce persons from their social and natural contexts" (Martin, 1984, pp. 179-183). First, all knowledge is interrelated and contextual. Thus, with connected knowing, piercing boundaries of specialization is emphasized such that knowledge is interdisciplinary. In this paradigm, there is a shift in pedagogy and epistemology. The relations of teaching and learning shift from learning information that has been designated as knowledge by authorities to the collective construction of knowledge. The teacher uses a problem-posing, dialogic approach as teacher and students search for knowledge together. Students become self-directed, reflective learners. Teacher and students engage in a relationship of reciprocity where both are equally committed to creating a context for learning. In a framework of connected knowing, cognitive and affective development are intimately related, and faculty are responsible for enhancing both. An institution of connected knowing legitimizes learning that takes place outside the classroom, recognizes multiple learning styles, and values learning grounded in experience. Institutions of connected knowing are connected institutions, embedded in reciprocal relations that link the university to the communities of which it is an integral part. Connected knowing treats education not as something separate from life but as part of life. Thus, education becomes a lifelong process.

A framework of connected knowing embraces moral education. Trained intelligence may lead to ethical reasoning, but it is only in the convergence of the cognitive and the affective that commitment and purpose in active engagement emerges as the goal of education. Although connected knowing relies on relations and context in forming moral judgments, it is a standard of justice in a democratic community that suggests an ethics of care to guide moral reasoning. Thus, connected knowing espouses a morality of subjective understanding based on care. Caring represents a quest for understanding (Noddings, 1984). Moral education aims at an ethic of caring, of meeting the other in a moral relation, forming the foundations of a connected and engaged citizenry.

A shift toward a paradigm of connected knowing has sweeping and deep implications for altering the institutional culture of higher education. It also has profound implications for student development education (Fried and Associates, 1995). Connected knowing affirms the relation of affective development to cognitive development, thus placing the student affairs professional in an overtly educational role. Connected knowing legitimizes out-of-classroom experiences as a significant locus for learning, thus recognizing the importance of the learning environment traditionally defined as the responsibility of student affairs. Connected knowing allows student development educators to go beyond consideration of professional ethics in relations with students and to become themselves moral educators (Kitchener, 1985). That student affairs professionals should be concerned with ethics has been amply affirmed and articulated in the American College Personnel Association's *Statement of Ethical Principles and Standards* (1993), and more recently in the *Student Learning Imperative* (1994). The latter argues forcefully for student affairs professionals to consider themselves educators who are concerned with connected knowing and learning outside the classroom. Because of the centrality of moral education to a paradigm of connected knowing, moral education is also central to the function of student development education. Morality in moral education affirms that those responsible for this aspect of education relate morally to all involved. Kitchener's principles have particular relevance here because they are intended to guide professional behavior. But it is personal ethics, the means by which a person plans, designs, and facilitates moral education, that enhances an ethic of caring for students so that they learn how to relate to others morally and continue to do so.

Education for an Ethic of Caring

Education that impels students toward the formation of values is experiential by nature. It must be centered on relationships and connections in practice. As Noddings explains, "moral decisions are, after all, made in situations; they are qualitatively different from the solution of geometry problems" (1984, p. 96). Ethical education should provide "apprenticeships for caring" aimed toward experience that enhances a "sense of relatedness, of renewed commitment to receptivity" (1984, p. 190). This kind of education is stifled by a process of teaching and learning where knowledge is distanced from the learner, objectified, abstracted, and analytical. Ethical education embraces knowledge from a constructivist perspective in which "all knowledge is constructed, and the knower is an intimate part of the known" (Belenky, Clinchy, Goldberger, and Tarule, 1986, p. 136). This orientation to knowledge does not negate the importance of reason for ethical consideration, but instead emphasizes a convergence of affective and cognitive development. Neither blind sentiment nor unfeeling rationalization must dominate. Cognition and affect must combine to create "ethical affect," integrated thinking about ethical issues (Noddings, 1984, p. 171). John Dewey explained this convergence of theory and practice, knowledge and moral conduct, in this way: "The level of action fixed by *embodied* intelligence is always the important thing" ([1927] 1946, p. 210). Although objectification distances what is known from one's experiences, constructivist approaches to knowledge connect, in an intimate way, "ways of knowing with habits of being" (hooks, 1994, p. 43).

Community Service Learning as Connected Knowing

One experiential approach, known as community service learning (CSL), can provide powerful opportunities for ethical apprenticeships based on relatedness, receptivity, and responsiveness. Community service learning is a pedagogy of reflective inquiry linking students' affective and cognitive development and connecting institutions of higher education to communities of which they are a part. Jane Kendall defines CSL in this way: "Service-learning programs emphasize the accomplishment of tasks that meet human needs in combination with conscious educational growth. . . . They combine needed tasks in the community with intentional learning goals and with conscious reflection and critical analysis" (Kendall, 1990, p. 20).

Over the past twenty-five years community service learning has found justification in educational institutions as both an alternative pedagogy and a movement aimed at transforming the culture of American higher education (Barber and Battistoni, 1993; Barber, 1992; Kendall, 1990). Ernest Boyer has placed community service at the core of the creation of the "New American College," what he describes as "an institution that celebrates . . . its capacity to connect thought to action, theory to practice" (Boyer, 1991, p. A18). For Boyer, the university as a "connected institution" would have students learn and teachers teach in a way that is responsive to community concerns. Similarly, Robert Coles has advocated connecting community experience to purposive academic study (1989). "Our colleges and universities," writes Coles, "could be of great help to students engaged in community service if they tried consistently and diligently to help students connect their experiences in such work with their academic courses. Students need more opportunity for moral and social reflection on the problems that they have seen at first hand . . . students need the chance to directly connect books to experience, ideas and introspection to continuing activity" (1994, p. A64).

Recent research indicates that CSL should be emphasized by student development educators as a way in which, as the *Student Learning Imperative* suggests, they "can intentionally create the conditions that enhance student learning and development" (American College Personnel Association, 1994, p. 1). There is evidence that students who engage in community service activity as part of their education make greater gains in moral reasoning than those who do not. CSL enhances moral sensitivity, increases students' sense of civic responsibility, and increases their sensitivity to issues of racial prejudice (Myers-Lipton, 1996; Boss, 1994). Engaging in care for the welfare of another human being helps students define themselves as effective moral agents.

The findings of the Higher Education Research Institute's research on student development indicate that interest in service learning is rapidly growing. Institutions with a strong research orientation and narrowly specialized curricula show a decline in student service activities. This trend is alleviated by student enrollment in interdisciplinary courses and by student-faculty interaction around topics that integrate living and learning (Astin, 1991, 1996).

These findings indicate that CSL is likely to thrive at institutions of connected knowing and that it is likely to be inhibited at institutions of separate knowing. At institutions of connected knowing, CSL has the potential not only of offering educational opportunities that develop an ethic of purpose and compassion but also of fostering institutional collaborations between student affairs professionals and academic faculty. Such collaborations foster the convergence of affective and cognitive development necessary for developing higher levels of moral judgment.

Ethics Education in Theory

A theoretical expression of CSL has been proposed by Delve, Mintz, and Stewart (1990). Their *service learning model* includes elements of Perry's cognitive development model, Kohlberg's moral development model, and Gilligan's moral judgment model drawing on theoretical work on women's psychological development. The service learning model incorporates these developmental frameworks into an experiential learning model drawing on the contributions of Dewey, Lewin, Piaget, and Kolb (see Figure 5.1). Kolb posits a cycle of learning that begins with *concrete experience.* The subsequent quadrants of the cycle are labeled *reflective observation, abstract conceptualization,* and *active experimentation,* leading to new occurrences of concrete experience. The four steps in the cycle describe learning abilities that interact with one another to form distinct learning styles (Kolb, 1984, 1985). The Delve, Mintz, Stewart service learning model parallels Kolb's, which has a five-phase cycle progressing from exploration to *clarification,* to *realization, activation,* and *internalization,* with the intent to bring together into a single theoretical scheme the development of learning abilities and the development of values. In Kolb's experiential learning model, each quadrant of the cycle represents a learning style formed by the interaction of learning abilities; the learner is defined as a *Diverger, Assimilator, Converger,* or *Accomodator.*

Kolb emphasizes the development of values in his learning model by enriching the feeling-thinking dialectic with that of value-fact, and by doing the same with the acting-observing axis such that it expresses a meaning-relevance dialectic (Figure 5.2). The four learning styles relate to four virtues—*love, justice, wisdom, and courage*—governed by the overarching virtue *integrity.* What Kolb's model highlights is that learning styles embody not only how one knows, but what one does with what one comes to know. In the learning process CSL connects knowledge and moral behavior. "By engaging in deliberate and planned service interventions," assert Delve, Mintz, and Stewart, "students are challenged to clarify and act on their values" (1990, p. 39). To accomplish this as a goal of education requires a transformation of the role of the educator and the curriculum.

The service learning model incorporates the work of Gilligan and Kohlberg on moral development. Gilligan (1982), along with other relationally oriented authors, asserts a responsibility orientation in contrast to Kohlberg's (1969)

Figure 5.1. Comparison of Kolb's Experiential Learning Cycle with the Service Learning Model

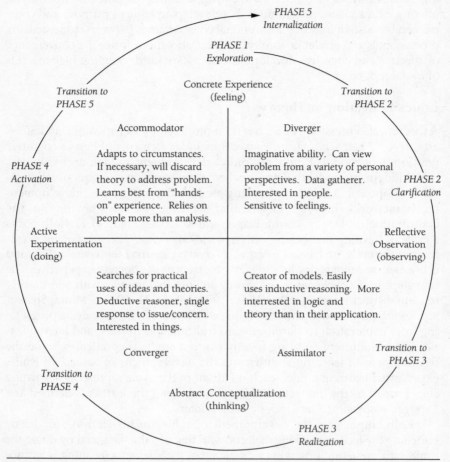

Source: Delve, C. I., Mintz, S. D., and Stewart, G. I. (eds.). *Community Service as Values Education.* New Directions for Student Services, no. 50. San Francisco: Jossey-Bass, 1990, p. 37.

rights orientation to morality. Gilligan approaches moral issues not as intellectual problems that can be solved by abstract reasoning, using hierarchical principles and arriving at logical conclusions, but "as concrete human problems to be lived and solved in living . . . reasons point to feelings, needs, situation conditions, and (the) sense of personal ideal rather than universal principles and their applications" (Noddings, 1984, pp. 96-97). In a responsibility orientation, the individual resolves conflicts by trying to understand each person's needs, goals, and perspective and then suggesting the best possible solution for all involved. "For constructivists, the moral response is a caring response" (Belenky, Clinchy, Goldberger, and Tarule, 1986, 149).

Figure 5.2. Values in Kolb's Experiential Learning Cycle

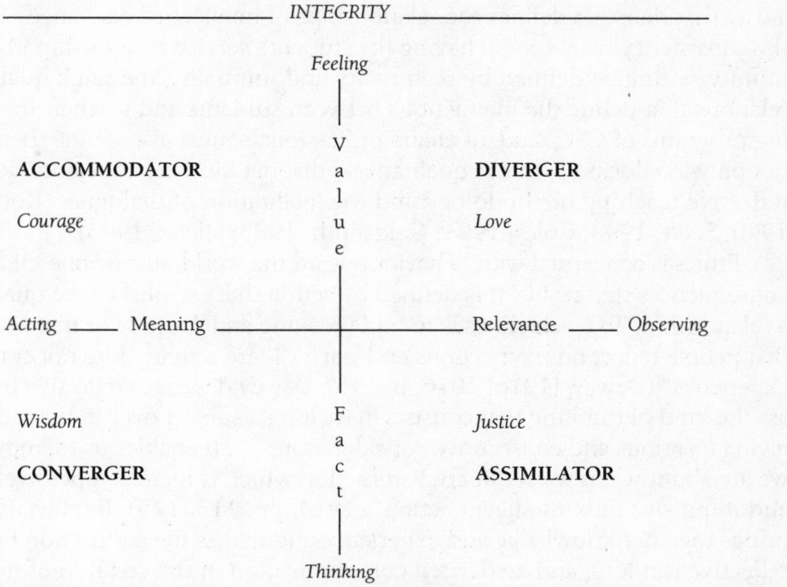

```
_____ INTEGRITY _____

                        Feeling
                          |
                          V
    ACCOMMODATOR          a           DIVERGER
                          l
                          u
      Courage             e            Love

  Acting ____ Meaning ____|____ Relevance ____ Observing

      Wisdom              F           Justice
                          a
    CONVERGER             c          ASSIMILATOR
                          t
                          |
                        Thinking
```

Source: Delve, C. I., Mintz, S. D., and Stewart, G. I. (eds.). *Community Service as Values Education.* New Directions for Student Services, no. 50. San Francisco: Jossey-Bass, 1990, p. 40.

In a constructivist approach to experience, "the moral and spiritual dimension[s]" of one's life become areas for reflection as precursors to translating "moral commitments into action, both out of a conviction that 'one must act' and out of a feeling of responsibility to the larger community in which [one] live[s]" (Belenky, Clinchy, Goldberger, and Tarule, 1986, p. 150). Boss's findings seem to affirm the theoretical basis of the service learning model, pointing out that it is plausible that gains in moral reasoning result from the "convergence of social disequilibrium *and* cognitive disequilibrium," and that "one's fullest potential in moral reasoning comes about through a successful integration of the Kohlbergian justice (cognitive) and more feminine care (social/affective) perspectives" (1994, p. 191). CSL provides an opportunity for student affairs professionals to "engage our students in the clarification of values so that care becomes the motivation for individual, meaningful behavior, and for change to be deliberate and just" (Delve, Mintz, and Stewart, 1990, p. 41).

Ethics Education in Practice

Learning theory can guide us into an educational orientation that provides for an apprenticeship of caring, yet there remains the question of how we practice an education centered on relationships, receptivity, compassion, reciprocity, and mutuality. Our practice must be consistent with the guiding theory, and in the case of CSL, the practice is defined primarily by a process of reflective inquiry and dialogue. The educator's role is to facilitate reflection on experience in such a way that dialogue defines the relationships of intellectual exchange. There is the consistency here, too, of having the student's service relationship in a community setting be defined by reciprocity and mutuality, the same qualities of relations that define the interactions between students and teacher. In designing programs of CSL, student affairs professionals must also define themselves not only as educators, but as qualitatively distinct kinds of educators skilled in reflective teaching methodology and the facilitation of dialogue. (Kottcamp, 1990; Scott, 1993; Coles, 1994; Goldsmith, 1995; Silcox, 1993).

Ethics is concerned with behavior toward the world outside oneself and the consequences that result. It is defined by action that establishes the qualities of a relationship. To teach ethics is to find meaning and purpose in that action, so that people reflect on their actions and learn. "Mere activity does not constitute experience" (Dewey, [1916] 1976, p. 146). Dewey describes reflective thinking as "the kind of thinking that consists in turning a subject over in the mind and giving it serious and consecutive consideration. . . . It enables us to know what we are about when we act. It converts action which is merely appetitive, blind, and impulsive into intelligent action" (1910, pp. 113, 125). Intelligent action brings together knowledge and experience and makes the connection between reflective thinking and associated communication in the creation of meaning from experience. Reflection, in Dewey's use of the concept, implies that experience must be articulated in order for it to be communicated ([1916] 1976).

The essence of reflective inquiry is its ability to make connections between all the various pieces of information that accompany a problematic situation *and* to make the connection between intent and result of conduct. First, information becomes "*knowledge* only as its material is *comprehended*," wrote Dewey, "and understanding, comprehension, means that the various parts of information acquired are grasped in their relation to one another-a result that is attained only when acquisition is accompanied by constant reflection upon the meaning of what is studied" (1910, p. 177). Second, Dewey defined reflection as the "intentional endeavor to discover specific connections between something which we do and the consequences which result, so that the two become continuous" ([1916] 1976, p. 151). Finally, Dewey observed that "the effects of connected action forces men to reflect upon the connection itself" ([1916] 1976, p. 24). Reflective inquiry is at the core of service learning, creating meaning out the service experience.

For example, consider a sociology sophomore participating in a community service learning program. During the first week's seminar, when asked to reflect on both her motivations for wanting to be involved in a shelter for homeless women and the reasons that women ended up in the shelter, her reply was that it did not matter to her how the women became homeless, she just wanted to do what she could to help them. She responded confidently and with conviction, according to her feelings; her caring, subjective, intuitive capabilities. Four weeks later she was asked the very same question. This time she explained that she spent more time than any of the other advocates in finding out the circumstances that led to the women coming to the shelter. Her motivation had not changed, but the social context of the problem of homelessness was enriched by reflection that connected the subjective knowledge of her experience with the objective knowledge of her discipline; her affective development was enlarging her cognitive development and the convergence had impelled her toward personal and professional commitment and purpose.

Reflection is fostered in a pedagogical context of relationships and connections defined by dialogue. It is "dialogue and exchange of views [that] allows each individual to be understood on his or her own terms" (Burbules, 1993). The process of dialogue becomes training for receptivity. It changes how students relate to each other in the process of learning. The process of objective knowing that has dominated higher education, in abstracting and impersonalizing knowledge, has established a process of learning associated with "discussion," not dialogue. "The primary purpose [of discussion] is . . . to manipulate the listeners' reactions, and . . . see the listener not as an ally in conversation but as a potentially hostile judge" (Belenky, Clinchy, Goldberger, and Tarule, 1986, p. 108). Dialogue, in contrast, "cannot be reduced to the act of one person's 'depositing' ideas in another," notes Freire, "nor can it become a simple exchange of ideas to be 'consumed' by the discussants" (1994, pp. 69, 70).

Multiculturalism, Dialogue, and Ethics. Consider how this process relates to the specific issue of multiculturalism in higher education. Dialogue shaped by the context of experience in the community allows for the sensitivity and reciprocity of multicultural education that respects and honors the social reality and experiences of diverse groups of people students encounter. The context of the community transforms the dialogue into an inclusive learning experience. This experience creates a connected classroom in which individual perspectives and private truths are respected and transformed into public knowledge by sharing, listening, and stretching to understand across differences of life experience (Belenky, Clinchy, Goldberger, and Tarule, 1986). By implication, the educational process is as important as its content. Focus on the process of dialogue, reflection, and community context suggests an affirmation of multiculturalism that is different from one based on the composition of the student body or an alteration of topics in the curriculum. This position does not argue against a curriculum that offers courses addressing a range of cultures or against exposing students to different cultures. It suggests that both these means of addressing multicultural education can be enhanced by education that instills receptivity and reciprocity in the process of learning. It is fundamentally based on an understanding of knowledge as dependent on perspective and context and the creation of knowledge as creation of a joint set of understandings. Meyers refers to this as "culture as a foundational philosophy," a way in which "to actively pursue diverse ways of knowing and to acknowledge the wider spectrum of experience" (1995, p. 12). It is the basis for an ethics of caring. "Caring involves stepping out of one's own personal frame of reference into the other's. When we care, we consider the other's point of view, his objective needs, and what he expects of us. Our attention, our mental engrossment is on the cared-for, not on ourselves" (Noddings, 1984, p. 24).

Journal Reflections. Students involved in community service need the opportunity to "reflect on what they are doing, what they would like to be doing, and what they are having difficulty doing" (Coles, 1993, p. 147). One tool of reflection is the personal creation of knowledge through journal writing (Goldsmith, 1995). If we conceive of ethical development emerging from the dialectical struggle, deeply individual and personal, between fact and value, knowledge and feeling, in a particular situation, we can conceive of a journal as the place where students can actively engage in working out these struggles. It is in the act of confronting and naming these struggles that learning emerges. Journals also connect the private and the public; although journal writing is a private act, the sharing of reflective inquiry brings one's private reflection into a context of shared knowing. "Training for receptivity involves sharing and reflecting aloud. It involves a kind of close contact that makes personal history valuable" (Noddings, 1984, pp. 121–122).

Journal writing and reflection are enriched by storytelling as a way of collectively constructing what is known and being receptive to others' ways of knowing. Stories are inherently relational and contextual. Coles has emphasized the importance of stories in drawing out the convergence of cognitive and affective development in the experience of community service. In sharing experiences through storytelling as reflective individuals—with the skills of receptivity and the abilities of listening and understanding—we construct our ethical identities. We use stories to see how people perceive themselves in relation to others and their social context. Through stories, people unlock the basis of their values and commitments. In sharing stories, new interpretations are revealed that can clarify one's own experience in relation to others. The stories do not necessarily have to be about service. Coles believes that "stories are a means of glimpsing and comprehending the world," and "service is a means for putting to use what has been learned, for in the daily events designated as service, all sorts of stories are encountered and experienced" (1993, p. xxiii). How we know ourselves and others through our stories and how we come to know through the stories of others opens the way for discovering our identity as moral agents.

Ethics, Service, and Justice

Through CSL, student development educators can provide opportunities for students to develop purpose and compassion in their life practices. They can also approach education in such a way that they can find purpose in their teaching. Consider Dewey's observation that "to put ourselves in the place of another, to see things from the standpoint of his aim and values, to humble our estimate of our own pretensions to the level they assume in the eyes of an impartial observer, is the surest way to appreciate what justice demands in concrete cases" ([1932] 1981, p. 251). Asserting the value of justice as a defining quality of one's relationships with others also asserts a larger educational aim. I want to suggest two things here: first, that the quality of the service relationship is as important as the relationship itself, and second, that the purpose of education in America is participation in the life of a democratic culture. I am referring here to the distinction Sidney Hook drew between "the morality of the task" and "the task of morality" (quoted in Noddings, 1984, p. 179). In any discussion of moral development or educational method, there is a larger frame of reference defined by participation in a democratic community. As John Dewey made clear, "unless education has some frame of reference it is bound to be aimless, lacking a unified objective. The necessity for a frame of reference must be admitted. There exits in this country such a unified frame. It is called democracy" (Dewey, 1981, p. 415). Democracy defines the purpose for our actions and for education. How we conceive of reciprocal and mutual relations in a democratic culture contributes to our compassion for others through a lens of justice. Ethics becomes a matter of the quality of our relationships with others defined by caring. Compassion and moral behavior—justice and caring—are the means; the end is a democratic culture. "Justice as an end in itself," Dewey advised, "is a case of making an idol out of a means at the expense of the end which the mean serves" ([1932] 1981, p. 249).

As student affairs professionals reflect on their practice as ethics educators, they might consider the distinction Dewey drew between the qualities of justice and charity relationships. In his *Ethics* he presents a justice orientation that "looks at the well-being of society as a whole," "realizes the interdependence of interests," is "fixed upon positive opportunities for growth," and is "centered on social rights and possibilities." This he contrasted with a "charity" perspective that "assumes a superior and inferior class," is "negative and palliative merely," and that treats "individuals as separate, to whom, in their separateness, good is to be done" ([1908] 1976, p. 349). The aim of service types of activity is "general social advance, constructive social reform, not merely doing something kind for individuals who are rendered helpless from sickness or poverty. Its aim is the equity of justice, not the inequality of conferring benefits." "Charity may even be used as a sop to one's conscience while at the same time it buys off the resentment which might otherwise grow up in those who suffer from social injustice" (Dewey, [1932] 1981, p. 301). He concludes his thoughts on service in *Ethics* with the observation that "the best kind of help to others, whenever possible, is indirect, and consists in such modifications of the conditions of life, of the general level of subsistence, as enables them independently to help themselves" ([1908] 1976, p. 350).

Shifting the Paradigm

Education can best encompass purpose and compassion through a paradigm of connected knowing. Ethics education is, in fact must be, experiential—it is defined by relationships and connections and the quality of those relationships. A paradigm of connected knowing redefines the role of education for everyone concerned in the learning process. The experience of relating with others through community service uncovers dimensions of justice in a democratic culture.

Finally, a word of caution that can serve as an inspiration during these times of wrenching tensions and transformations on college campuses. My note of caution has to do with a seemingly casual repetition of the notion of a "paradigm shift" in higher education to the point where overuse of the concept may have trivialized its meaning. History indicates that a paradigm exists because it offers a model for approaching problems and solutions, has a coherent tradition and historical perspective, and serves a community function. Adopting a new paradigm may be instigated by a crisis situation in which a community recognizes an acute problem. "The decision to reject one paradigm is always simultaneously the decision to accept another," notes Thomas Kuhn, "and the judgment leading to that decision involves comparison of both paradigms with nature and with each other" (1970, p. 77). But it also requires more; it is a decision that "can only be made on faith," since "the competition between paradigms is not the sort of battle that can be resolved by proofs" (1970, p. 148). Crisis alone is not enough. Without faith in the efficacy of the alternative orientation, I and my co-contributor, David Sundberg, would suggest, we will at best find higher education in a situation that Matthew Arnold described as "wandering between two worlds, one dead, the other powerless to be born" (Arnold, [1867] 1962, p. 876).

References

American College Personnel Association, Standing Committee on Ethics. "Statement of Ethical Principles and Standards." *Journal of College Student Development,* 1993, *34,* 89-92.

American College Personnel Association. *The Student Learning Imperative: Implications for Student Affairs.* Washington, D.C.: American College Personnel Association, 1994.

Arnold, M. "Stanzas from the Grande Chartreuse." In M. Abrams (ed.), *The Norton Anthology of English Literature.* Vol. 2. New York: W. W. Norton, 1962. (Originally published 1867.)

Astin, A. W. *What Matters in College? Four Critical Years Revisited.* San Francisco: Jossey-Bass, 1991.

Astin, A. W "Involvement in Learning Revisited: Lessons We Have Learned." *Journal of College Student Development,* 1996, *37* (2), 123-148.

Barber, B. *An Aristocracy of Everyone: The Politics of Education and the Future of America.* Oxford, U.K.: Oxford University Press, 1992.

Barber, B., and Battistoni, R. "A Season of Service: Introducing Service Learning into the Liberal Arts Curriculum." *PS: Political Science and Politics,* June 1993, *26,* 235-262.

Belenky, M., Clinchy, B., Goldberger, N., and Tarule, J. *Women's Ways of Knowing.* New York: Basic Books, 1986.

Boss, J. "The Effects of Community Service on the Moral Development of College Ethics Students." *Journal of Moral Education,* 1994, *23* (2), 183-198.

Boyer, E. "Creating the New American College." *Chronicle of Higher Education,* March 9, 1991, p. A18.

Burbules, N. *Dialogue in Teaching: Theory and Practice.* New York: Teachers College, Columbia University, 1993.

Coles, R. *The Call of Service.* New York: Houghton-Mifflin, 1993.

Coles, R. *The Call of Stories.* New York: Houghton-Mifflin, 1989.

Coles, R. "Putting Head and Heart on the Line." *Chronicle of Higher Education,* Oct. 26, 1994, p. A64.

Delve, C. I., Mintz, S. D., and Stewart, G. I. (eds.). *Community Service as Values Education.* New Directions for Student Services, no. 50. San Francisco: Jossey-Bass, 1990.

Dewey, J. *The Public and Its Problems.* Chicago: Gateway, 1946. (Originally published 1927.)

Dewey, J. *Democracy and Education.* Vol. 9 of *The Middle Works of John Dewey.* Carbondale: Southern Illinois University Press, 1976. (Originally published 1916.)

Dewey, J. *Ethics.* Vol. 5 of J. Boydston (ed.), *The Middle Works of John Dewey.* Carbondale: Southern Illinois University Press, 1976. (Originally published 1908.)

Dewey, J. *Education and Social Change.* In *The Later Works of John Dewey.* Vol. 11. Carbondale: Southern Illinois University Press, 1981.

Dewey, J. *Ethics.* Vol. 7 of *The Later Works of John Dewey.* Carbondale: Southern Illinois University Press, 1981. (Originally published 1932.)

Dewey, J. *How We Think.* In *The Later Works of John Dewey.* Vol. 8. Carbondale: Souther Illinois University Press, 1986. (Originally published 1910).

Freire, P. *Pedagogy of the Oppressed.* New York: Continuum, 1994.

Fried, J., and Associates. *Shifting Paradigms in Student Affairs.* Washington, D.C.: American College Personnel Association, 1995.

Gilligan, C. *In a Different Voice.* Cambridge, Mass.: Harvard University Press, 1982.

Goldsmith, S. *Journal Reflection: A Resource Guide for Community Service Leaders and Educators in Service Learning.* Washington, D.C.: American Alliance for Rights and Responsibilities, 1995.

hooks, b. *Teaching to Transgress: Education as the Practice of Freedom.* New York: Routledge, 1994.

Kendall, J. (ed). *Combining Service and Learning: A Resource Book for Community and Public Service.* 2 vols. Raleigh, N.C.: National Society for Internships and Experiential Education, 1990.

Kitchener, K. "Ethical Principles and Ethical Decisions in Student Affairs." In H. J. Canon and R. D. Brown (eds.), *Applied Ethics in Student Services.* New Directions for Student Services, no. 30. San Francisco: Jossey-Bass, 1985.

Kohlberg, L. "Stage and Sequence: The Cognitive Developmental Approach to Socialization." In D. A. Goslin (ed.), *Handbook of Socialization Theory and Research.* Skokie, Ill.: Rand McNally, 1969.

Kolb, D. *Experiential Learning.* Englewood Cliffs, N.J.: Prentice Hall, 1984.

Kolb, D. *Learning Styles Inventories.* Boston: McKerr, 1985.

Kottkamp, R. "Means for Facilitating Reflection." *Education and Urban Society,* 1990, 22 (2), 182-203.

Kuhn, T. *The Structure of Scientific Revolutions.* (2nd ed.) Chicago: University of Chicago Press, 1970.

Martin, J. *Changing the Educational Landscape: Philosophy, Women, and the Curriculum.* New York: Routledge, 1984.

Meyers, M. "A Cultural Imperative for Wilderness Adventure Programs: A Native Hawaiian Example." *Journal of Experiential Education,* 1995, 17 (3), 11-15.

Myers-Lipton, S. "Service Learning: Theory, Student Development, and Strategy." In M. Ender (ed)., *Service-Learning and Undergraduate Sociology.* Washington, D.C.: American Sociological Association, 1996.

Noddings, N. *Caring: A Feminine Approach to Ethics and Moral Education.* Berkeley: University of California Press, 1984.

Scott, J. "A Journal Workshop for Coordinators." In J. Howard (ed.), *Praxis II: Service Learning Resources for University Students, Staff, and Faculty.* Ann Arbor, Mich.: Office of Community Service Learning, 1993.

Silcox, H. *A How To Guide to Reflection: Adding Cognitive Learning to Community Service Programs.* Philadelphia: Brighton Press, 1993.

JOHN SALTMARSH is associate professor at Northeastern University with a joint appointment in the Department of History and the Department of Cooperative Education.

Nonintrusive measures such as photographs of bulletin boards, architecture, graffiti, and other elements of the physical environment can provide a very accurate assessment of the ethical climate on campus.

Assessing the Campus' Ethical Climate: A Multidimensional Approach

James H. Banning

What is the ethical climate on today's campuses? What approaches are available to campuses to address this question? Can the assessment of the ethical climate lead a campus to function more ethically? These questions are important and timely. A headline in the *Chronicle of Higher Education* in 1989 read: "Rash of Ethical Lapses Spurs Colleges to Study Their Moral Responsibilities" (Magner, 1989). The article highlighted the all-too-familiar lapses stemming from widespread university misconduct in intercollegiate athletics, admissions, hiring practices, scientific research, economic development, and affirmative action practices and among faculty. In addition to the frequent newspaper coverage of these events, entire books attacking the moral and ethical behavior of the universities have been written, including *ProfScam* (Sykes, 1988), *Personal Fouls* (Golenbock, 1989), *Killing the Spirit* (Smith, 1990), and *Saints and Scamps* (Cahn, 1993). After highlighting new initiatives on the horizon to improve the ethical climate, Magner (1989, p. A11) noted that "attempts by colleges and universities to examine their own ethics have generally been weak and sporadic."

One reason campuses find it difficult to make solid attempts is that they have historically focused on ethical decisions residing at the level of an individual decision maker. It is at the individual level that our professional communities publish ethical rules in the form of professional codes (Kitchener, 1985) to help the decision maker perform ethically. When decisions are complex and involve conflicts among the codes, then Kitchener (1985) suggested that individuals invoke a set of ethical principles to help guide and justify decisions. When ethical principles are in conflict, a discussion of ethical theories provides a way of proceeding.

Canon (1989) suggested a similar approach, but placed more emphasis on the importance of the community or social environment in understanding and resolving conflict among ethical principles. There are approaches that allow for ethical discussions to occur at the community level and not just at the level of the individual. This chapter develops a general framework and matrix for assessing ethical behavior from a campus perspective and illustrates how the method of visual anthropology can be used to implement the matrix.

Approaching Ethical Behavior at the Community Level

Looking at ethical behavior at the institutional or campus community level is complex, but at least three approaches for judging ethical behavior at this level are viable: an ethical principles approach (Kitchener, 1985; Canon and Brown, 1985; Delworth and Seeman, 1984; Noddings, 1984), aggregating individual decisions to a campus summary; a fulfillment of community values approach (Brown, 1985); and a community change process approach (Huebner and Banning, 1987; Kelman and Warwick, 1978).

Ethical Principles Aggregation Approach. The ethical principles aggregation approach uses the ethical principles that have been developed to judge individual decision making. Kitchener (1985) offered a list of five principles that can be used to judge decisions: respecting autonomy, doing no harm, benefiting others, being just, and being faithful.

Respecting autonomy focuses on the notion that individuals have the right to decide what choices they want to make. As long as their actions or choices do not interfere with the welfare of others, their right to act and have freedom of thought and choice should be protected and cherished. *Doing no harm* speaks to the point that there is an obligation on all to avoid inflicting either physical or psychological harm on others and to avoid actions that might put others at risk. *Benefiting others* addresses the obligation to improve the welfare of others, even when such actions may cause an inconvenience for the person offering assistance. *Being just* focuses on the need to treat people equally, to afford each individual her or his rightful share. *Being faithful* includes the need to keep promises, tell the truth, be loyal, and maintain civility in human affairs.

The work of Delworth and Seeman (1984), Gilligan (1982), and Noddings (1984) suggested the additional ethical principle of caring. Noddings (1984) pointed out that the topic of ethical behavior is usually discussed largely from the perspective of a "hierarchical picture" where the language spoken is that of the father. Noddings (1984, p. 1) called for the mother's voice where "human caring and the memory of caring and being cared for" can serve as a foundation for ethical responses. Looking at the summary or total of all campus decisions from the perspective of these six principles would form the basis of the ethical principles aggregation approach to assessment at the institutional or campus level.

Fulfillment of Community Values Approach. A second approach in judging ethical behavior at the campus community level is derived from the work of Brown (1985). It is the fulfillment of values approach and is based on the notion that a campus's ethical behavior can be judged on how well it fulfills its selected set of values and goals. Brown (1985) suggested the following community values for institutions of higher education: peace issues, vocation as calling, developmental progress for all, theory and research, and a humane learning environment. The more recent work of Boyer (1990) suggested campus community goals of a purposeful community, an open community, a just community, a disciplined community, a caring community, and a celebrative community. An individual campus usually develops its own unique set of values and goals, which are generally derived from or are a part of the institutional mission statement. State university catalogues typically include instructional objectives, a philosophy of student character development, and policies regarding nondiscrimination and personal abuse. This information could be reformatted as statements of values or goals, for example, pursuit of academic excellence, pursuit of creativity, pursuit of diversity, pursuit of equal opportunity, and pursuit of an environment free from personal abuse. The fulfillment of the community values approach to understanding a campus's ethical climate basically asks the question, Is the institution fulfilling its stated goals and values? By combining the values approach with the ethical principles approach, not only should the campus be fulfilling its stated goals and values, these goals and values should be in concert with the basic ethical principles outlined by Canon (1989), Kitchener (1985), and Noddings (1984).

Community Change Process Approach. The community change process approach focuses on the process by which community decisions are reached or judgments are finalized and asks the question, Was the process an ethical one? Kelman and Warwick (1978) suggested several questions that need to be addressed when looking at a community or institutional change process from an ethical perspective. These include: who will participate in the process, how will diverse interests be represented, who will benefit or not benefit from the change, by what means will the decision for change be implemented (coercion, manipulation, persuasion, or facilitation), and finally, who will be assessing the ongoing consequences of the change? The community change or process approach can be added to the two previous approaches and by using all three of the approaches, the ethical questions at the campus level become: is the community fulfilling its stated values, is there adherence to ethical principles, and is the implementation process reflecting an ethical change process?

Importance of the Tripartite Approach. The following scenario illustrates that the choice of approach used in assessing campus behavior can lead to different conclusions regarding the judgment of ethical behavior. The scenario also underlines the importance of a framework that includes all three approaches in order to enhance the ethical climate of the campus. The situation is as follows: a vice president for student affairs at a Rocky Mountain university instructed the campus bookstore manager to remove *Playboy, Playgirl,* and *Penthouse* magazines from the shelf and to discontinue subscriptions. It was a decision by the vice president based on the knowledge of the relationship between pornography and violence against women and children. The campus had a strong personal abuse policy, which stated that abusive treatment of individuals on a personal or stereotyped basis would be prohibited. From both an ethical principles stand-point and a community values fulfillment standpoint, the behavior of the vice president appeared to be ethical. The decision, however, failed to meet the cri-teria of the community process approach. No dialogue occurred, and as a result, another extremely important principle was not considered, that of freedom of speech. The issues around the decision were not discussed with students, fac-ulty, or administrators. No outside input was sought. From the community process standpoint the decision was ethically flawed. If additional values had been sought in the decision-making process, the important issues of freedom of speech and respecting the autonomy of others perhaps would have surfaced with greater clarity and significance.

Understanding the ethical climate of a campus community involves know-ing what ethical principles an institution espouses, the values and goals it seeks to fulfill, and the processes by which the goals and values are achieved. This tripartite approach to understanding the ethical climate speaks to the initial question posed at the beginning of this chapter, namely, What strategies are available to address the ethical climate at a campus or institutional level? The question that remains to be answered is the second introductory question: Can the assessment of the ethical climate lead a campus to function more ethically?

Nontraditional Approach to the Assessment of Ethical Climate

A traditional approach to the assessment of ethical climate would stem from a deductive paradigm in which a set of ethical principles or institutional values would probably be selected for the development of a survey. The survey would then be sent to members of the campus community asking them to report their perceptions of institutional behavior by answering a variety of questions tap-ping the dimensions of ethical behavior. This approach is not seriously flawed, but it is time-consuming, obtrusive, and the issue of self-reporting bias because of social desirability factors is always present. A nontraditional approach to the assessment of campus ethical climate can be developed from a more inductive approach using a method from the discipline of anthropology.

The methods and strategies associated with anthropological research are becoming valued strategies for understanding institutions of higher education (Conrad, Neuman, Haworth, and Scott, 1994; Fetterman, 1991). A strong move-ment to more inductive, qualitative, and anthropological approaches to under-standing a campus community is also evident in student services (Banning, 1991, 1992, 1993; Kuh, 1993; Kuh and Whitt, 1988, Stage, 1992; Tierney, 1996).

Important to understanding the campus community from an anthropo-logical perspective is the concept of *artifact*. Artifacts, the created objects of our culture, communicate powerful and important messages (Hormuth, 1990). Kuh and Whitt (1988) and Whitt (1993) documented the importance of insti-tutional artifacts as communicators of campus culture. Kuh and Whitt (1988, p. 16) stated that cultural assumptions and beliefs "are just below the surface of conscious thought, are manifested in observable forms or artifacts." Geertz (1973) also captured the importance of artifacts as communicators of culture by suggesting that artifacts store cultural meaning. Can issues relating to ethical principles, fulfillment of values, and ethical change processes show up in campus physical artifacts such as art, signs, graffiti, and architecture? If so, can the methods associated with visual anthropology serve as the foundation for assessing campus ethical climate?

Visual Anthropology

Qualitative data-gathering methods typically fall into three classes: observations, analysis of documents, and interviews. Obtaining photographs of campus artifacts captures all three methods. A photograph captures an observation and becomes a document for analysis, and if the notion that a picture is worth a thousand words has merit, then the photograph is a brief interview as well. Photography is widely used to record data in visual anthropology. Visual anthropology is a relatively recent area of anthropological specialization (Seymour-Smith, 1986). The intent of visual anthropology is to study human behavior through a variety of photographic methods including the use of still cameras, movie cameras, and, more recently, the video camera. Collier described the camera as an instrument that captures a cultural slice of reality (1967) and photography as a method for removing the facade from human organizations and looking directly at their contents (Collier and Collier, 1986). Can photographs lead to an understanding of complex campus or institutional issues like *ethical climate?*

Recent work points to an affirmative response. Younge, Oetting, Banning, and Younge (1991) used photographs to assess the treatment philosophies of drug and alcohol abuse programs. In a statewide sample, photographs were taken of drug and alcohol treatment environments to capture how artifacts in the treatment facility communicated nonverbal messages regarding treatment philosophy. Messages regarding commitment to medical model, role of socioeconomic status in provision of services, and staff values toward clients were all ascertained from the photographs of artifacts in the treatment settings. For example, the agencies that served clients of lower socioeconomic status provided the clients with less control over their environment than those agencies serving a higher socioeconomic group. This was inferred from photographs of the facilities' heating and cooling thermostats. Photographs of the thermostats in the high-control environments showed the thermostats were off-limits to the clients and often locked by padlock. The opposite was found in those agencies serving clients of the higher socioeconomic group. They did not secure the thermostats, and photographs showed the absence of devices to limit client control. Banning (1991, 1993, 1995) used photographs of physical artifacts taken from the pedestrian environments of parks, malls, and campuses to illustrate messages relating to multiculturalism, including messages regarding women, gay men, lesbians, bisexuals, and the physically disabled.

Ethical Climate Assessment Matrix: Guidance for the Camera

If cameras and photographs are to be used to assess the ethical climate of the campus community, where do you point the camera? What artifact do you photograph? This dilemma reflects the modern research issue of identifying the most appropriate, least distorting relationships between the observer and the observed. Help is provided by Banning and Bartels (1993) in their presentation of a conceptual framework for using photos to conduct a cultural audit focusing on multicultural issues. The model can be adapted for use in assessing artifacts that give messages regarding the ethical climate of the campus. The Banning and Bartels (1993) model presents a four-dimensional matrix with the dimensions of type of artifact (art, signs, graffiti, and architecture); evaluative effect of the artifact (overtly positive to overtly negative); the content of the message being sent by the artifact (belonging, safety, equity, and role prescriptions); and multicultural parameter (gender, race, ethnicity, religion, sexual orientation, and disability).

The Banning and Bartels (1993) model can be transformed into an ethical climate assessment matrix (see Figure 6.1). The matrix has three dimensions: the type of physical artifact sending the message, the ethical issues dimension, and the evaluative effect or ethical saliency of the message.

Figure 6.1. Ethical Climate Assessment Matrix

Evaluative impact

Positive
Negative

Type of artifact

Art
Signs
Graffiti
Architecture

Ethical issue

Community change process
Goals
Targets
Means
Scope
Consequences

Ethical principles
Respect autonomy
Do no harm
Benefit others
Be just
Be faithful
Be caring

Fulfillment of values
Pursuit of academic excellence
Support of diversity
Provision of a humane environment
Developmental progress for all

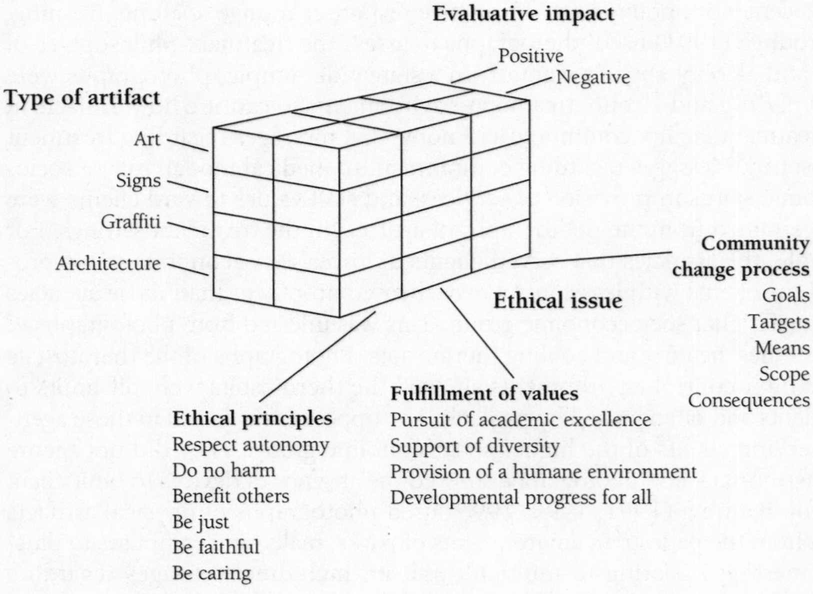

Types of Physical Artifacts on Campus. Artifacts are objects made by the people of a culture. They take a variety of forms, but in educational settings four categories are particularly important: *artifacts* include paintings, posters placed in campus buildings, and statuary work found on the campus landscape; *signs* fall into several categories, including official signs, unofficial signs, and illegitimate signs (Zeisel, 1975); *graffiti* is an illegitimate sign, but because of its ubiquitous nature on campus it warrants separate status in the classification system; *architecture,* or the physical structures of educational settings or classrooms, can also send important messages (Banning, 1992; Kuh, 1993; and Sturner, 1972).

Ethical Issues Dimension. Campus physical artifacts can encompass a number of ethical issues. The matrix presented uses the tripartite approach (ethical principles, fulfillment of values, and community change process) and the ethical questions imbedded in each approach. For example, in Figure 6.1 under the *ethical principles* approach are the categories respect autonomy, do no harm, benefit others, be just, be faithful, and be caring. In a similar fashion, under the *fulfillment of values* approach are listed some possible values. Each institution would have to develop the particular values and goals that would best represent the campus. Under the *community process* approach are listed the issues of choice of goals, definition of targets, choice of means, scope of participation, and assessment of consequences.

Evaluative Dimension. The evaluative effect or saliency of a physical artifact's message can be positive or negative. The negative message often stems from the judgment that the artifact produces a message that is contrary to the community's ethical value, such as the design and installation of unsafe ramps for wheelchairs. Physical artifacts can also send positive messages regarding ethical issues. These artifacts produce images that support the ethical values of the campus community. Examples of positive images might include art work that depicts the cultural heritage of various groups placed on display in a library. This type of display, positioned in a building used by most members of a college community, would be a positive message, in concert with campus commitments to the celebration of cultural diversity.

Implementation of the Matrix for Assessment of Campus Ethical Climate

The proposed matrix can be used to evaluate messages that convey the ethical climate of the campus. Using the matrix for the purpose of ethical climate assessment is similar to performing a culture audit. Whitt (1993) defined a culture audit as providing "both insiders and outsiders with a means to systematically discover and identify the artifacts, values, and assumptions that comprise an organization's culture" (p. 83). Whitt (1993) also suggested several principles to guide a culture audit: respect institutional culture, use multiple sources of information, and understand the importance of the role of the insider. When using the proposed matrix as a basis for an ethical climate audit, consideration of Whitt's (1993) principles is important.

Example One. A photograph was taken of some graffiti written along a passageway between two sections of a state university campus. The graffiti read "Nigger, Nigger, go home!" By using the dimensions of the matrix, the artifact can be classified. Its artifact type is graffiti. Its message relates to a number of ethical issues from each of the approaches: the artifact does do harm, it benefits no one, it is not just, and it is not caring; using the fulfillment of values approach, the artifact certainly does not advance such institutional goals as supporting diversity, creating a humane environment, or providing developmental progress for all; using the community change process approach, the designer of the artifact most likely did not include the participation of African Americans in the design process. Finally, the evaluative effect of the artifact in regard to the ethical dimensions outlined is clearly negative.

Example Two. At a large university, a picture was taken of a poster that showed a cartoon figure pointing a gun at a small child with the caption "Rush Phi Gamma Delta or we will shoot this kid." This fraternity rush poster fits into the matrix as well. The type of artifact is art/poster; the ethical issues touched by this photo are numerous: it does harm, it benefits no one, it is not caring, it does not create a humane environment, and it is supporting change by coercion and disregard for consequences for those not in power (children). The impact is negative.

Example Three. At a large university a picture was taken of what appeared to be a curb cut but was actually a glob of asphalt pushed up next to the curb. Again, this picture can fit into the matrix. The type of artifact is architecture; the ethical issues involved include not respecting the autonomy of students in wheelchairs, not being just or faithful to access, not supporting or valuing diversity, not providing developmental progress for all, and not providing for input from the user group. The effect is negative.

Example Four. A sign on a faculty member's door at a technical college reads "Do not knock—put materials under the door." This artifact type is a sign. The ethical issues involved could be several. Some students may be harmed by the unwelcoming message; the sign benefits only the designer. If the institution's goals include marketing the concept of the availability of faculty, then the sign does not indicate fulfillment or faithfulness. The sign, in terms of the change process, leaves little room for discussion or any doubt that the faculty member is in the power position. The effect is negative.

Example Five. A photograph of a poster of a menorah, signifying the Jewish holiday of Hanukkah, was taken at the window of an information desk in a residence hall. The artifact type is a poster. The ethical issues of benefiting others and fulfilling the institution's goal of support for diversity are present, and these messages would lead to a positive effect on the campus's ethical climate.

Example Six. A photograph was taken of a wrecked car that was placed in front of the campus student union just prior to spring break. It had been placed there to remind students of a recent student death due to alcohol consumption. The intended message was "don't drink and drive!" A graffiti writer chalked a confounding written message in front of the wrecked car: "Someone knew the driver of this car was homosexual." No one took the initiative to remove the offensive chalk message. The artifact type is a physical object, or structure. Several ethical issues come into play. The chalked message does do harm by its implied threat. It does not celebrate diversity, and certainly the gay, lesbian, and bisexual community did not participate in the presentation of the message. Its impact is negative.

Using the Matrix and the Camera to Enhance Campus Ethical Climate

The proposed matrix helps point the camera toward potential campus ethical issues. How can the photographs that result from this process lead to an enhancement of the campus's ethical climate? The linkage mechanism is community dialogue about the photographs. There will be both disagreements about where to point the camera and multiple interpretations of the ethical issues that are captured by the photographs. All parties do not have to agree on the interpretations of the photographs; movement toward an ethical community is based on the full participation of all campus community members in the discussion of differences and actions that should be taken or not taken regarding the messages of the photographs. To use Graff's (1992) perspective on multicultural education and the revitalization of American education, we need to allow the photographs to teach the controversy and raise the questions, not dictate the answers. It is through the debate about the meaning of the photographs that the ethical climate of the campus is revitalized. In controversy and dialogue, the principle approach to ethics is combined with the relational approach (Noddings, 1984), supporting the community change process approach and enhancing the probability of success. Kitchener (1985) made a similar point when she noted that ethical principles are often in conflict with one another when applied to real-life situations and suggested that discussion occur with other professionals for further understanding. In his work on how to design an ethics class, Prager (1993) concluded that it is the discussion around ethical issues that promotes enhanced understanding and that the "education lies in the debate, the exposure to a diversity of attitudes" (p. 32).

The dialogue around the issues identified through the use of the matrix and the photographs enhances the moral climate of the campus. The dialogue must, however, include all campus participants. Saskin (1984) held the position that organizations have an ethical imperative to do no intentional harm to members. He then reviewed the research that indicated a relationship between nonparticipatory structures in organizations and the following harm to employees: life span is shortened, coronary heart disease goes up, depression is present, alcohol abuse becomes a part of the picture, and productivity falls.

Conclusion

In order to enhance the ethical climate on a college campus, two key frameworks must be created: one for campus assessment and one for community dialogue around the ethical issues discovered by the assessment. A campus must agree that the difficult issues raised will be addressed in a climate of respectful speaking and listening (Palmer, 1987). The ethical climate assessment matrix presented in this chapter is one assessment framework that helps to direct the assessment activity. Within the framework of visual anthropology, the photographing of campus artifacts brings attention to ethical issues and stimulates community dialogue and change.

References

Banning, J. "Ethnography: A Promising Method of Inquiry for the Study of Campus Ecology." *The Campus Ecologist,* 1991, *9* (3), 1–4.

Banning, J. "Visual Anthropology: Viewing the Campus Ecology for Messages of Sexism." *The Campus Ecologist,* 1992, *10* (1), 1–4.

Banning, J. "The Pedestrian's Visual Experience on Campus: Informal Learning of Cultural Messages." *The Campus Ecologist,* 1993, *11* (1), 1–4.

Banning, J. "Campus Images: Homoprejudice." *The Campus Ecologist,* 1995, *13* (3), 3.

Banning, J., and Bartels, S. "A Taxonomy for Physical Artifacts: Understanding Campus Multiculturalism." *The Campus Ecologist,* 1993, *11* (3), 2–3.

Boyer, E. *Campus Life: In Search of Community.* Princeton, N.J.: The Carnegie Foundation for the Advancement of Teaching, 1990.

Brown, R. D. "Creating an Ethical Community." In H. J. Canon and R. D. Brown (eds.), *Applied Ethics in Student Services.* New Directions for Student Services, no. 30. San Francisco: Jossey-Bass, 1985.

Cahn, S. *Saints and Scamps: Ethics in Academia.* (Rev. ed.) Totowa, N.J.: Rowman and Littlefield, 1993.

Canon, H. J. "Guiding Standards and Principles." In U. Delworth, G. R. Hanson, and Associates, *Student Services: A Handbook for the Profession.* (2nd ed.) San Francisco: Jossey-Bass, 1989.

Canon, H. J., and Brown, R. D. *Applied Ethics in Student Services.* New Directions for Student Services, no. 30. San Francisco: Jossey-Bass, 1985.

Collier, J. *Visual Anthropology: Photography as a Research Method.* New York: Holt, Rinehart, and Winston, 1967.

Collier, J., and Collier, M. *Visual Anthropology.* Albuquerque: University of New Mexico Press, 1986.

Conrad, C., Neuman, A., Haworth, J., and Scott, P. (eds.). *Qualitative Research in Higher Education: Experiencing Alternative Perspectives and Approaches.* Needham Heights, N.J.: Simon & Schuster, 1994.

Delworth, U., and Seeman, D. "The Ethics of Care: Implications of Gilligan for the Student Services Profession." *Journal of College Student Personnel,* 1984, *25* (6), 489–492.

Fetterman, D. M. (ed.). *Using Qualitative Methods in Institutional Research.* New Directions for Institutional Research, no. 72. San Francisco: Jossey-Bass, 1991.

Geertz, C. *The Interpretation of Culture.* New York: Basic Books, 1973.

Gilligan, C. *In a Different Voice.* Cambridge, Mass.: Harvard University Press, 1982.

Golenbock, P. *Personal Fouls.* New York: Carroll & Graf, 1989.

Graff, G. *Beyond the Culture Wars: How Teaching the Conflicts Can Revitalize American Education.* New York: Norton, 1992.

Hormuth, S. *The Ecology of the Self.* Cambridge, U.K.: Cambridge University Press, 1990.

Huebner, L., and Banning, J. "Ethics of Intentional Campus Design." *NASPA Journal*, 1987, *25* (1), 28-38.

Kelman, H., and Warwick, D. "The Ethics of Social Intervention: Goals, Means, Consequences." In G. Bermant, H. Kelman, and D. Warwick (eds.), *The Ethics of Social Intervention*. New York: Wiley, 1978.

Kitchener, K. "Ethical Principles and Ethical Decisions in Student Affairs." In H. J. Canon and R. D. Brown (eds.), *Applied Ethics in Student Services*. New Directions for Student Services, no. 30. San Francisco: Jossey-Bass, 1985.

Kuh, G. (ed.). *Cultural Perspectives in Student Affairs Work*. Washington, D.C.: American College Personnel Association, 1993.

Kuh, G., and Whitt, E. *The Invisible Tapestry: Cultures in American Colleges and Universities*. ASHE-ERIC Higher Education Report, no. 1. Washington, D.C.: Association for the Study of Higher Education, 1988.

Magner, D. "Rash of Ethical Lapses Spurs Colleges to Study Their Moral Responsibilities." *The Chronicle of Higher Education*, Feb. 1989, pp. A11–A13.

Noddings, N. *Caring: A Feminine Approach to Ethics and Moral Education*. Berkeley: University of California Press, 1984.

Palmer, P. "Community, Conflict, and Ways of Knowing." *Change*, 1987, *19* (5), 20–25.

Prager, R. "Designing an Ethics Class." *Educational Leadership*, 1993, *51* (3), 32–33.

Saskin, M. "Participative Management Is an Ethical Imperative." *Organizational Dynamics*, 1984, *12*, 4–22.

Seymour-Smith, C. *Dictionary of Anthropology*. Boston: G.K. Hall, 1986.

Smith, P. *Killing the Spirit*. New York: Penguin, 1990.

Stage, F. (ed.). *Diverse Methods for Research and Assessment of College Students*. Alexandria, Va.: American College Personnel Association, 1992.

Sturner, W. "Environmental Code: Creating a Sense of Place on the College Campus." *Journal of Higher Education*, 1972, *43*, 97–109.

Sykes, C. *ProfScam: Professors and the Demise of Higher Education*. New York: St. Martin's Press, 1988.

Tierney, W. "An Anthropological Analysis of Student Participation in College." In F. Stage, G. Anayaa, J. Bean, D. Hossler, and G. Kuh (eds.), *College Students: The Evolving Nature of Research*. Needham Heights, N.J.: Simon & Schuster, 1996.

Whitt, E. "Making the Familiar Strange: Discovering Culture." In G. Kuh (ed.), *Cultural Perspectives in Student Affairs Work*. Washington, D.C.: American College Personnel Association, 1993.

Younge, S., Oetting, E., Banning, J., and Younge, K. "Psychological Messages from the Physical Environment: The Drug and Alcohol Treatment Center Environment." *International Journal of the Addictions*, 1991, *25* (7A, 7B), 905–955.

Zeisel, J. *Sociology and Architectural Design*. New York: Russell Sage Foundation, 1975.

JAMES H. BANNING is professor in the School of Education at Colorado State University and partner and consultant in Campus Ecology Services in Santa Fe, New Mexico.

*What do webs, chopsticks, and forks have to do with ethics? They
provide us with metaphors for understanding the evolving modes of
ethical inquiry that must be created if we are to transform our ethical
beliefs and practices to meet the needs of our increasingly complex,
multicultural campuses.*

Next Steps and Emerging Possibilities

Jane Fried

Shortly after the explosion of TWA flight 800, I flew from Chicago to Cleveland. The security in the O'Hare airport was high, as was the anxiety of many
of the soon-to-be passengers. The man sitting next to me on the plane grasped
his rosary beads intensely and prayed all the way from take-off to landing. The
flight was very bumpy and became increasingly frightening for me. Shortly
before arrival, the man took out a NASA identification card, which he was
wearing around his neck on a chain. When I inquired, he told me that he was
a NASA engineer who had been one of those responsible for piecing together
a plane that had crashed in Pittsburgh several years before. He was still having
nightmares. A NASA engineer haunted by nightmares of a plane crash, clutch-
ing to his faith and his rosary beads! In my "intentional world" (Shweder,
1991) engineers do not pray about airplanes; they have faith in science. God's
place in the mechanics of flight is marginal at best. This engineer's faith in God
and lack of faith in mechanical flight was unsettling to me; terrifying, considering his profession. According to Fritjof Capra, noted physicist, systems ana-
lyst, and mystic, "Whenever the essential nature of things is analyzed by the
intellect, it will seem absurd or paradoxical" (1988, p. 33). I believe that it is
not coincidental that the engineer I encountered appeared to be of Mexican
ancestry. His intentional world was different from mine, and in his, there
seemed to be no conflict between faith in science and faith in God.

In the old paradigm ethical system, which I described earlier in this book,
science and faith tend to be considered mutually exclusive categories. Decisions made by logical, rational thinking tend to have higher credibility than
those arrived at by intuition. Principles guide thinking, reason prevails over
emotion, empirical data are privileged over wisdom or contextual patterns and
values; ethical decisions are made accordingly. Strong arguments are logical

107

arguments. Storytelling is considered anecdotal. Storytelling can be powerful and convincing, but in the old paradigm belief system, stories relate particular situations and particularities make weak arguments. Stories are taken literally, not metaphorically.

Many of the ideas presented in this book require the reader to shift from old paradigm ethical thinking, in which general principles prevail and universal notions of right and wrong are presumed to exist. At the present time, student affairs practitioners are working in environments where many different ethical and belief systems guide individual behavior. The ability to maintain awareness of several belief systems simultaneously has become a survival skill (Parry and Doan, 1994). Both intellectual and emotional flexibility are necessary to maintain professional effectiveness in this environment. The ethical practitioner must retain an awareness of his or her beliefs about relationships, teaching, learning, and work while simultaneously remaining open to other ideas about these key areas of professional life. In this process, stories, metaphors, and proverbs serve us well. They can provoke a shift in awareness from logic and linear thinking to intuition and circular or weblike insight. They make us more aware of the connectedness of events, people, places, and activities. Stories show us that we are part of a whole, that the story, the teller, and the listener are part of a web of meaning makers. "The stories are always bringing us together, keeping this whole together. . . . 'Don't go away, don't isolate yourself, but come here, because we have all had these kinds of experiences.' And so there is this constant pulling together to resist this tendency to run or hide or separate oneself during a traumatic emotional experience. This separation not only endangers the group but the individual as well—one does not recover by oneself" (Silko, 1996, p. 52). What are we, as groups of professionals who aspire to community, trying to do together in higher education? Is that a good question with which to begin our discussion of ethics? Is there a better one (Greenleaf, 1991)?

The interconnectedness of all experience, the need for communities to remain in contact with all members, even those who have ignored or defied community expectations, is a frequent theme in the stories of many cultures. These cultures emphasize the need to weave every experience, both painful and joyful, into a wisdom web. A Buddhist aphorism asserts, "No one is my friend; no one is my enemy; everyone is my teacher." The Navajo remind us of the integrity of all life and experience in this poem (Zona, 1994, p. 40):

> I have been to the end of the earth.
> I have been to the end of the waters.
> I have been to the end of the sky.
> I have been to the end of the mountains.
> I have found none that are not my friends.

The metaphor of the web has spun itself through our professional literature in recent years, complementing, if not replacing our traditional architectural metaphors such as foundations, building blocks, and capstones. Surfing the Internet web has become a metaphor for our emerging ability to speak with any other connected person or access any other connected source of information throughout the world. Fritjof Capra has asserted that physical "reality" is actually a weblike process rather than a series of solid objects or fundamental building blocks. "The material universe is seen as a dynamic web of interrelated events. None of the properties of any part of this web is fundamental; they all follow from the properties of the other parts, and the overall consistency of their interrelations determines the structure of the entire web" (1988, p. 51). Capra predicts that science will replace its allegiance to foundational metaphors with notions of the web, or network, in which everything is connected to everything else, and no particular aspect of the web is considered fundamental.

The web metaphor applies equally well to ethics. As part of our collective effort to replace either/or thinking with both/and thinking, we must be able to focus on the parts of a problem or ethical dilemma as well as the whole, on general principles and virtues that are specific to a particular campus. My colleague Cathy Bao Bean refers to this process as the *chopstick or fork dilemma*. Cathy was raised by Chinese immigrant parents in post-World War II New Jersey, an area that was filled with immigrants and their children from all over the world. Her adult intellectual life is Anglo American and is conducted in English. Her early emotional life is Chinese and was conducted in Mandarin. Her mothering skills, learned both from her mother and from American friends and relatives, include both Chinese and American customs. She intentionally raised her son to be bicultural. She is fully conscious of the many connected parts of her life: the emotional, intellectual, spiritual, ethical, and material. The chopstick or fork dilemma refers to the process of knowing which level of awareness and which set of skills are appropriate to use in any given situation.

Naming this dilemma "chopstick/fork" allows us to recognize it more quickly when it appears, but it does not give us guidelines by which we can make judgments about what type and level of response might be effective or appropriate in a particular situation. When a practitioner becomes aware of the numbers of ethical, perceptual, and meaning-making systems that may be in operation in any specific situation, it is easy to revert to a dualistic attitude to preserve one's sense of security. One may either view the situation as chaotic and random and thus become absolved from any responsibility, or construe it as one that must be placed under control by a responsible person, either oneself or another person into whose jurisdiction this problem falls on the organizational chart.

A brief example of a possible situation is as follows: Carolyn, an African American woman, was hired to direct fall orientation, which occurs in September; open houses for recruitment, which occur in October; and residence hall staff training, which has an intense period of activity in late August and then continues periodically throughout the fall semester. Carolyn was interviewed in April when she was four months pregnant. She expected to deliver in mid-September. She did not tell her potential employer that she was pregnant and was under no legal obligation to do so. She took the job, which began in mid-July, and fully expected to deliver her baby and continue to do her work, with a little delegating for about three weeks in mid-September. This campus did not have a waiting period for maternity leave, so she was entitled to the leave immediately. Shortly after her arrival on campus her colleagues realized that she was pregnant. An intense, behind-the-scenes debate began about the ethics of her failure to inform the new employer of her condition at the time she was offered the job. No one discussed the situation with Carolyn. She worked as she had intended, and began to make plans for delegating some of her responsibilities during her anticipated three-week absence. By the time orientation began, all plans were in place for the three areas of her responsibility, and staff had been given the necessary operational responsibilities. Although there were no conversations about the situation between Carolyn and her colleagues, many of them harbored ill feelings, which made it difficult for them to appreciate the quality of her work or the extra effort she made prior to delivery to ensure that all programs would take place effectively.

This situation raises many questions about multiple ethical systems in operation simultaneously. How much autonomy does the staff member have in this new position? Did she harm either the institution or her colleagues by not informing them in advance of her pregnancy? This institution was very interested in increasing the number of staff members of color. In this case, would the desire for more staff diversity have taken precedence over the new person's three-week absence at a very demanding time of year? Who was entitled to make the choice about priorities? If we examine this dilemma from the perspective of virtue ethics, which virtues prevail in shaping behavior? Prudence, integrity, respectfulness, and benevolence all might play a role in determining how to handle the problem whenever it became a problem and for whomever it was a problem. Carolyn wanted this job, and the committee considered her the best candidate in the pool. When Carolyn weighed her possible disclosure of pregnancy, which choice would have been the more prudent for her—the one that enhanced her chances of securing this position, thereby achieving professional advancement and helping her family, or the one in which she disclosed the pregnancy and risked losing the opportunity? Could she be sure that a white employer would be respectful of her promise to meet all her commitments? Does race matter in this situation? Race matters to the white employer who wants more people of color. Does it or should it matter to Carolyn and her family? The pregnancy may have been much more of a problem for the previously employed staff members than for Carolyn. She had made arrangements for support and child care well before her delivery date and had numerous family members living close by. She knew she would have to overcome early exhaustion and the conflict between staying home with the baby and going back to work so soon after delivery. On the other hand, her grandmother had lived with her family, and her mother's maternity leaves were typically three or four weeks long. Her husband planned to stay at home for at least two weeks after she returned to work. Since none of her new colleagues asked, no one realized how Carolyn's family was involved in this process and how she expected to manage all her responsibilities. A very obvious dilemma is the question of when we choose to discuss our concerns with a colleague and when we remain silent. What really is none of our business and when is a situation like a pregnancy simultaneously public and private? If we begrudge our colleague the right to make this decision privately and then judge her without sharing our concerns, have we acted ethically?

There are dilemmas within dilemmas in this situation. They pertain to ethical principles and different ideas about virtue. They also pertain to race, culture, and socioeconomic status. The assumptions of middle-class white or Latino staff members about privacy, family, the relationship between work and family, roles for men and women within the family, and managing the tensions between family and work may or may not be the same as the assumptions Carolyn and her family held and on which they based their decisions about work, residence, birth, gender roles, and caretaking. Carolyn and her family may or may not hold the values that have come to be considered typical for middle-class African American families. There are no clear answers about what Carolyn "should" have done. Every answer depends on which set of assumptions the questioner considers most valid in these circumstances.

It seems that most ethical dilemmas must now be addressed by examining the interactions between means and ends, principles and context, and people and their responsibilities. Asking ourselves and each other what we are trying to do as a learning community becomes fundamental to the ethical dialogue. Everything we do teaches somebody something. We teach by our words, our policies, our relationships, and our actions. These teaching, learning, and deciding processes create multiple webs of meaning for all members of our communities. Our learning communities have become complex, continuously evolving open systems that are generally in states of disequilibrium. Although disequilibrium is unsettling, uncomfortable, and unpredictable, it is also a major indicator of vitality. The system constantly exchanges energy with its environment and is itself evolving toward higher levels of complexity (Caple, 1987). In ethics as in many other fields, traditional ideas of evolution are changing from predictability to indeterminacy. "Indeterminacy is the freedom available at each level, which, however, cannot jump over the shadow of its own history. Evolution is the open history of an unfolding complexity, not the history of random processes. What emerges are the contours of a world in which little (if anything) is purely random, but much is undetermined and shaped by a creativity that transcends the systems which are its vehicles" (Jantsch, 1982, p. 352). In such structures, near equilibrium often appears to be destroyed, but far equilibrium seems to emerge as perspective shifts and events unfold (Caple, 1987).

Both in our understanding of evolutionary systems and in the metaphor of the web, change is constant. No single element is fundamental. Many elements interact simultaneously as evolution stumbles forward in unpredictable ways. This evolutionary process has been observed and tracked on the atomic level and the biological level as well as societal and institutional levels (Capra, 1982, 1988). Colleges and universities are not exempt from this process, although our ideologies of progress do not predispose us to describe change in this way. The authors and the editor of this book have presented a range of perspectives on various topics of ethical concern to professionals in student affairs and other areas of the academy. We remain convinced that ethical thinking and ethical behavior are part of a continuous teaching, learning, and deciding process in constant evolution. We also believe that the dilemmas facing our profession have forced us to move beyond our traditional reliance on old paradigm, principle-centered thinking and toward more complex dialogues and matrices for ethical decision making. We have explained how such dialogues can occur between and among various segments of the higher education community, how complex ethical reflection can be used in management settings, how ethics can be integrated into experiential and service learning, and how ethical climates can be assessed nonintrusively through the use of visual artifacts and analytic matrices.

Attention to ethics and the ethical consequences of decisions should be increased at this time because of the complexity of our campuses. No set of ethical assumptions can be presumed to prevail in any situation. Assumptions should be questioned and precedents reexamined. Perhaps higher education should follow the example set by hospitals and some corporations and establish ethics review committees. More productively, colleges and universities should consider establishing ethics pre-view committees to discuss ethical problems on an ongoing basis or conduct ongoing staff and faculty development programs on ethical decision making in a complex world. At the very least, members of the student affairs profession can elevate their own awareness of the ethical implications of their daily activities and decisions. We can use a variation of Rion's (1989) checklist and ask ourselves, Why am I so concerned about this problem? Whose interests are affected by the resolution? Whose problem is it? Are there ethical principles or virtues involved? If so, which group, from which culture? What decision can I make that honors my own beliefs and also respects the beliefs of others involved? Finally, we can again ask ourselves, in the words of Robert Greenleaf (1991), what we are trying to do in higher education.

Campus communities have become too complex to make the search for universal ethical guidelines feasible or desirable. Dialogue among people of good will can support an evolutionary process of ethical thinking and acting that creates and maintains learning communities where respect flourishes, differences are used to deepen understanding, and wisdom and knowledge in their many forms can coexist and enrich each other. If my seatmate on the flight from Chicago to Cleveland had been my colleague on campus, we might have had a fascinating conversation about the connections he makes between faith and science and the disconnections that were so much more apparent to me. We would have used the luxury of our setting, an institution dedicated to investigating ideas, and the luxury of our mutual educational purposes to understand and learn from each other. We might have come away from the conversation with more understanding or with new confusions and perplexities. We would have increased our awareness of possibilities never before considered. And we certainly would have strengthened our own awareness of the connection between facts and relationships, wisdom and knowledge, principles and virtues, people and ideas.

References

Caple, R. "The Change Process in Developmental Theory: A Self-Organization Paradigm, Part 1." *Journal of College Student Personnel,* 1987, *28* (2), 100–104.

Capra, F. *The Turning Point: Science, Society, and the Rising of Culture.* New York: Simon & Schuster, 1982.

Capra, F. *Uncommon Wisdom.* New York: Bantam Books, 1988.

Greenleaf, R. *Servant Leadership.* New York: Paulist Press, 1991.

Jantsch, E. "From Self-Reference to Self-Transcendence: The Evolution of Self-Organization Dynamics." In W. Schieve and P. Allen (eds.), *Self-Organization and Dissipative Structures.* Austin: University of Texas Press, 1982.

Parry, A., and Doan, R. *Story Re-Visions: Narrative Therapy in the Postmodern World.* New York: Guilford Press, 1994.

Rion, M. *The Responsible Manager.* Amherst, Mass.: HRD Press, 1989.

Shweder, H. *Thinking Through Cultures.* Cambridge, Mass.: Harvard University Press, 1991.

Silko, L. *Yellow Woman and a Beauty of the Spirit.* New York: Simon & Schuster, 1996.

Zona, G. *The Soul Would Have No Rainbow If the Eyes Had No Tears.* New York: Simon & Schuster, 1994.

JANE FRIED is associate professor in the Department of Health and Human Services at Central Connecticut State University and is former chair of the Standing Committee on Ethics of the American College Personnel Association.

INDEX

Ordering Information

New Directions for Student Services is a series of paperback books that offers guidelines and programs for aiding students in their total development—emotional, social, and physical, as well as intellectual. Books in the series are published quarterly in Spring, Summer, Fall, and Winter and are available for purchase by subscription as well as individually.

Subscriptions cost $52.00 for individuals (a savings of 35 percent over single-copy prices) and $79.00 for institutions, agencies, and libraries. Standing orders are accepted. New York residents, add local sales tax for subscriptions. (For subscriptions outside the United States, add $7.00 for shipping via surface mail or $25.00 for air mail. Orders *must be prepaid* in U.S. dollars by check drawn on a U.S. bank or charged to VISA, MasterCard, or American Express.)

Single copies cost $20.00 plus shipping (see below) when payment accompanies order. California, New Jersey, New York, and Washington, D.C., residents, please include appropriate sales tax. Canadian residents, add GST and any local taxes. Billed orders will be charged shipping and handling. No billed shipments to post office boxes. (Orders from outside the United States *must be prepaid* by check drawn on a U.S. bank or charged to VISA, MasterCard, or American Express.)

Shipping (single copies only): one issue, add $5.00; two issues, add $6.00; three issues, add $7.00; four to five issues, add $8.00; six to seven issues, add $9.00; eight or more issues, add $12.00.

All prices are subject to change.

Discounts for quantity orders are available. Please write to the address below for information.

All orders must include either the name of an individual or an official purchase order number. Please submit your order as follows:
   Subscriptions: specify series and year subscription is to begin
   Single copies: include individual title code (such as SS55)

Mail all orders to:
   Jossey-Bass Publishers
   350 Sansome Street
   San Francisco, California 94104-1342

For subscription sales outside of the United States, contact any international subscription agency or Jossey-Bass directly.